# 5
## ingredients
# 10
## minutes

For my favourite musician, GB,
at whose table I wish to grow old.

## about the author

Jules Clancy is a food lover – the type of girl who plans her holidays around restaurant reservations. She is a full-time blogger, food scientist, writer and photographer. After graduating in food science from university, Jules worked in product development for Kellogg, then travelled the world making wine. Back home in Sydney, she took a job designing chocolate biscuits. Discovering the world of food blogs, Jules became hooked, invested in a digital camera and started her own blog (www.thestonesoup.com). She now makes a living blogging and running the Stonesoup Virtual Cookery School, which teaches people from all over the world to cook quick, healthy, delicious food. Jules lives in the beautiful Snowy Mountains of Australia with her fiancé GB. When she's not cooking or writing about food she can be found indulging her passions for red wine, red shoes and blue cheese.

# 5
## ingredients
## 10
## minutes

*Delicious, healthy recipes
for tired and hungry cooks*

# JULES CLANCY

## WITH PHOTOGRAPHY BY JULES CLANCY

MICHAEL JOSEPH
*an imprint of*
PENGUIN BOOKS

# welcome

Hello and welcome! Firstly, I just wanted to say a big thank you for picking up a copy of my book. I really appreciate your support.

There are a few things you should know about me right from the start: I *love* food, especially veggies, and I have very high standards when it comes to what I cook and eat. I also love simplicity. So I am constantly on the look-out for ways to make my cooking less complicated and time-consuming without sacrificing deliciousness or healthiness. In the next few pages I'll explain a bit more about the 5 ingredients–10 minutes concept and how it can help you. But first, let's set the scene . . .

In my last job, I had an hour commute each way. And that was on a good day. I can't tell you how soul-destroying it was to get into my car at the end of a long, stressful day and know I had at least an hour ahead of me, jockeying with thousands of other commuters, before I'd be home safe. And then I'd have to figure out what to cook for dinner . . . Sometimes I'd stop on the way home to pick something up. Often I'd find myself wandering the aisles, looking for inspiration. With so much choice, decision became incredibly difficult. Sound familiar?

One of the biggest challenges we all face when it comes to cooking is being tired at the end of a long day. And hungry. And having to turn around and get something on the table that is not only fast and healthy, but tastes good too. Bit of a tall order, right? So that's where *5 Ingredients 10 Minutes* can help. It is designed to come to the rescue when the 'What's for dinner?' question crosses your mind.

In this book you'll find delicious, healthy recipes that can be made in minutes, most with at least 4 variations to suit pretty much all dietary requirements, or just for fun. If you haven't already done so, I'd love it if you became a regular reader of my blog. Just pop over to www.thestonesoup.com and sign up for my weekly email newsletter with more recipes and tips . . . it's free.

Happy cooking!
With love,

Jules x

# about 5 ingredients

Like my blog, Stonesoup, this book is about fresh, healthy, delicious food. Food that tastes good and is also good for us. The fact that the recipes in this book contain 5 ingredients and can be made in 10 minutes is a bonus.

As I am constantly discovering, when you strip food back to the essentials and let the ingredients speak for themselves, it can only mean great things from a flavour perspective. Throw in a healthy dose of veggies and you can't go wrong when it comes to healthy eating. Don't let anyone, especially those cheffy types, convince you that you need 'layers of flavour' and an ingredients list as long as your arm to create delicious food. That's one style of cooking that can taste great if someone else is preparing it and cleaning up.

For home cooking, I believe that keeping the number of ingredients and the steps involved to a minimum is where it's at. As I was writing this book, I constantly challenged myself to come up with the most delicious recipes possible while sticking to my ingredient limit. I can't tell you how many times the end results amazed and even shocked me with the complexity of flavour, given the limited number of ingredients.

Don't let the simplicity of these recipes fool you into thinking they aren't going to taste amazing. If they didn't make my taste buds sing, they wouldn't be here. If you're sceptical, I understand, but if you give them a go you'll be pleasantly surprised at what you can create with only 5 ingredients.

There are a few recipes that don't use the whole 5, so don't stress if there are only 4 or 3 ingredients. And of course I'm not going to be looking over your shoulder if you choose to add a few extra bits and pieces – by all means go for it!

To keep it realistic, the '5 ingredients' do not include salt, pepper, olive or other cooking oil. Since most recipes will use all 3 of these, I'm expecting them to be in your pantry.

# about 10 minutes

It's a fact of modern life that most people don't have hours to prepare elaborate meals every day. Even though I love cooking, I also find myself struggling to make time. I chose 10 minutes as a limit because I wanted to demonstrate that healthy cooking doesn't need to take much time. I mean, you can't even get pizza delivered in 10 minutes.

Part of keeping my recipes speedy is choosing methods that are as quick as possible. The other piece of the puzzle is making the most of convenient ingredients where appropriate. Don't worry, I'm not going to suggest you use frozen chicken nuggets or other highly processed foods; I'm talking about using canned chickpeas rather than soaking and cooking from scratch, and grilled aubergine and peppers from the deli instead of charring them at home.

The '10 minutes' is just a guideline for how long each recipe will take. Everyone cooks at a different speed, depending on their level of skill and personal style, so some people may take a little longer than others. I always time myself to make sure it's only taking me 10 minutes, but I cook quickly and with gas. So I put out a challenge on my blog (www.thestonesoup.com) to see whether the idea of a 10-minute recipe is realistic for regular home cooks. I got a fabulous response and most people were able to keep within the 10-minute limit. A few did take a little longer, but they recognised that if they made the dish again, they'd be able to meet the time challenge. So don't feel discouraged if it takes you longer on your first attempt. By the second or third time you should be meeting the 10-minute challenge very comfortably.

To help you get there as quickly and effortlessly as possible, I've included a few 'time tricks' with some of the recipes to help you get speedy results without stressing yourself out.

almonds

# snacks and starters

# warm mashed cannellini beans *with* parmesan

serves 2

- 1 clove garlic, finely sliced
- 400g can cannellini beans, drained
- large handful freshly grated parmesan
- lemon juice
- crusty bread, to serve

Cannellini beans and parmesan are a delicious combination. I often purée them in a food processor and serve them cold. But this warm version, mashed with a fork, is far more rustic and soul-warming with less washing up.

1. Heat a few tablespoons olive oil in a medium frying pan.

2. Cook garlic for a minute, or until starting to brown.

3. Add beans and cook for a few minutes, until they are warmed through.

4. Remove from the heat and mash beans with a fork.

5. Stir in cheese and a squeeze of lemon.

6. Taste and season, adding more lemon if you like. Serve with bread.

variations:

**Dairy-free:** skip the parmesan and serve drizzled with a good-quality, peppery extra virgin olive oil.

**Different beans:** replace the cannellini beans with butter beans, borlotti beans, kidney beans, chickpeas or lentils. Home-cooked beans work just as well. You'll need about 240g and remember to season generously.

**Vegan:** try the dairy-free option, or replace the parmesan with 2–3 tablespoons tahini (sesame seed paste).

**Short on time?** Forget the garlic and purée the beans in a food processor. Serve cold.

# beetroot 'pesto'

serves 4
as a light
snack

- 250g cooked beetroot, drained
- 1 clove garlic, finely chopped
- 50g pinenuts
- 80g parmesan, finely grated

I've been making beetroot 'pesto' for years, a brilliant idea where you use cooked beetroot instead of basil. I do prefer the fresh earthiness enough to roast the beets myself, but that would blow the 10-minute limit. Luckily, it's easy now to find cooked or canned beetroot in the supermarket. While it's quicker and easier to whizz this in a food processor, feel free to chop everything finely by hand if you have a minimalist food processor-free kitchen. It will take a little longer but will still be just as delicious.

1. Whizz the beets, garlic, pinenuts and cheese in a food processor until you have a chunky paste.

2. Add 6 tablespoons olive oil and whizz until just combined.

3. Taste and season well.

variations:

**If you've got more time:** to make home-roasted beets, trim and scrub beets, wrap in foil and bake at 180°C for 45 minutes to 1 hour or until beets are tender. Cool, then use as per the recipe. They will need more generous seasoning and possibly a tiny splash of vinegar.

**Vegan:** replace the parmesan with extra pinenuts.

**Different veg:** replace the beets with other cooked or roasted veg such as sweet potato or carrots.

**Budget:** replace the pinenuts with a less expensive nut like almonds or peanuts. Roasted cashew nuts are also lovely.

# red pepper *and* hazelnut dip

serves 4
as a snack

- 250g jar roasted red peppers, drained
- 1 clove garlic, finely chopped
- 200g roasted hazelnuts
- 1 tablespoon red wine vinegar
- 2 teaspoons smoked paprika

Inspired by one of my favourite Middle Eastern dips, muhammara, which is usually made with roasted red peppers, walnuts and pomegranate molasses. This quick version with hazelnuts and red wine vinegar is every bit as good.

I love this as a dip with pita or other bread, but it also makes a great sauce to spice up pork chops, sausages or even some lamb. As with the beetroot pesto on page 15, if you don't have a food processor, hand chopping the ingredients will give a suitably rustic result.

1. Whizz all ingredients in a food processor until you have a rough paste.

2. Add a few tablespoons extra virgin olive oil and process until just mixed.

3. Taste and season.

variations:

**Different nuts:** replace the hazelnuts with roast almonds, walnuts, pecans, pinenuts or cashews.

**Can't find smoked paprika?** Replace with regular paprika or leave it out altogether.

**Budget:** replace some or all of the nuts with fresh breadcrumbs, preferably from a good-quality sourdough loaf or pita bread.

**Nut-free:** replace the hazelnuts with breadcrumbs as above.

**Home-roasted peppers:** feel free to use your own home-charred and peeled.

# cream cheese, honey and soy crostini

- 4–6 slices crusty baguette
- cream cheese
- honey
- soy sauce

Before you start thinking I've gone a bit crazy, bear with me. I came up with this idea after having an amazing dinner at a little tapas joint in Barcelona. It was the type of place that was standing room only, with all the food prepared behind the bar. I had a great time trying things and watching the chef work his magic.

I couldn't believe it when I saw him spread some little rounds of bread with a soft, creamy cheese then drizzle over honey and finish it off with a dash of soy sauce. I was intrigued and just had to try it. It was a flavour explosion: sweet, salty, creamy. I highly recommend experiencing it yourself.

1. Generously spread baguette slices with cream cheese.

2. Drizzle each with about ½ teaspoon honey.

3. Finish with a tiny drizzle of soy sauce and freshly grated black pepper.

variations:

**Dairy-free/vegan:** replace the cheese, honey and soy with smashed avocado spiked with a little lemon or lime juice.

**Gluten-free:** replace the baguette with rice crackers or other gluten-free crackers. And make sure you're using a gluten-free soy sauce such as tamari.

**Soy-free:** be sparing with the honey and serve sprinkled with sea salt flakes instead of the soy sauce.

**Different cheese:** replace the cream cheese with a soft goat's cheese, creamy brie or freshly grated parmesan.

# marinated chorizo *with* rosemary *and* garlic

- ½ a small chorizo, finely sliced
- 1 small sprig rosemary
- zest of ½ a lemon
- 1 clove garlic, finely sliced
- crusty bread, to serve

This is a little like two starters in one. First you can eat the chorizo on its own and then you can use some bread to mop up the flavoured oil.

Be careful not to buy the fresh 'cooking chorizo', but the traditional dried chorizo that doesn't need cooking.

1. Place chorizo, rosemary, lemon zest and garlic in a small glass or jar.

2. Cover with good-quality extra virgin olive oil.

3. Serve immediately with crusty bread or allow to stand for a while.

variations:

**Vegan:** try marinating roast mushrooms like this.

**Different herbs:** replace the rosemary with thyme.

**Different sausage:** try any good-quality salami, especially the more spicy ones.

# tuna pâté with celery

serves 4
as a snack

- 185g can tuna in oil, drained
- 75g unsalted butter, softened
- juice + zest of ½ a lemon
- 2 anchovies, optional
- celery, to serve

I've always loved tuna in all its forms, especially the good-quality stuff out of a can that has been preserved in olive oil.

This is brilliant served with crunchy celery and is equally good with bread or crackers. I've also enjoyed it as a decadent sandwich filling accompanied by baby spinach leaves.

It's super quick to make in a food processor, but you need to make sure your butter is soft. If you don't have a food processor, just smash everything together with a fork. It will be chunky and rustic, but no less delicious.

1. Whizz tuna, butter, lemon juice and zest and anchovies in a food processor.

2. Taste and season. It may need a little more lemon juice.

3. Serve with celery sticks that have been sprinkled with salt and pepper.

variations:

**Dairy-free:** replace the butter with avocado.

**Vegan:** replace the tuna, butter and anchovies with the flesh of a ripe avocado.

**Fish-free:** replace the tuna and anchovies with a drained can of white beans such as cannellini or butter beans.

**No anchovies?** They really add depth of flavour but if you're not a fan, like my Irishman, just leave them out and be a little more generous with the salt.

# spiced pita chips

serves 2
as a snack

- 1 tablespoon smoked paprika
- 1 large round pita bread, sliced into thick ribbons

I first came across the idea of spicing and frying pita bread to make 'chips' for a salad. Since then I tend to keep some pita in the freezer in case I need a last-minute snack. While these chips are not the healthiest, they are delicious and at least you know exactly what has gone into them.

1. Preheat a wok or large frying pan on a very high heat.

2. Combine paprika with 3–4 tablespoons olive oil and season well.

3. Toss pita ribbons in the oil to coat. Stir-fry for a few minutes, until the bread is crisp and brown.

4. Sprinkle with salt. Serve hot or at room temperature.

variations:

Can't find smoked paprika? Replace with regular paprika or use 1 teaspoon or less of chilli powder instead. It's also lovely with a little ground cumin and coriander or the Lebanese spice blend baharat.

Gluten-free: replace the pita with rice crackers, skip the toasting and just serve with the spiced oil for dipping.

More substantial: serve with things like hummus or baba ghanoush.

Short on time? Skip the cooking and serve the spiced oil with commercial corn chips.

10-minute trick:
Make sure you get your
wok on to heat first thing.

# soups

# courgette *and* basil soup

- 2 cloves garlic, finely sliced
- 4 medium courgettes, grated, diced or sliced
- 750ml vegetable stock
- 2 handfuls grated parmesan + shaved parmesan, to serve
- small bunch basil, leaves picked

This soup varies depending on my mood. Sometimes I coarsely grate the courgette, other times I dice it. If I'm in the mood for something more chunky, I slice it into coins.

1. Heat a few tablespoons olive oil in a large frying pan.

2. Cook garlic over a medium-high heat for about 30 seconds, until starting to brown.

3. Add courgettes and cook, stirring frequently, for about 6 minutes or until the vegetables are starting to soften.

4. Add stock and bring to the boil.

5. Add grated parmesan and basil.

6. Taste, season and serve with extra parmesan shavings on top.

## variations:

**Vegan/dairy-free:** just skip the parmesan and serve with a generous drizzle of extra virgin olive oil or chilli oil.

**Different veg:** replace the courgettes with fresh or frozen peas, or broccoli. Adjust the cooking time to suit the veg.

**No vegetable stock?** Replace with half chicken stock and half water so the chicken stock doesn't overpower the courgette flavour.

**More substantial:** toss in a drained can of chickpeas or white beans, or handful of shredded, bought barbeque chicken.

**Different herbs:** basil is my favourite here, but flat-leaf parsley or mint will also work well.

10-minute trick:

Boil the stock in a separate saucepan while
the courgettes are cooking to save time.

# broccoli *and* green curry soup

- 250ml coconut milk
- 3–4 tablespoons green curry paste
- 2 heads broccoli, chopped into tiny trees
- 2–3 tablespoons peanut butter

While I prefer fresh broccoli, this soup is also great made with frozen; just pop it straight in the pan – it shouldn't take much longer to cook and will save you the chopping step. When chopping fresh broccoli, I like to finely slice most of the stems and add them to the pot so I minimise waste.

1. Heat a large saucepan on a high heat. Add a few tablespoons of cream from the top of the coconut milk or some oil. Stir-fry the curry paste for 15–30 seconds or until you notice the aroma. Be careful not to burn.

2. Quickly add 2 cups water and the coconut milk. Bring to a simmer.

3. Add broccoli. Bring back to a simmer and cook uncovered for 7–8 minutes or until the broccoli is tender.

4. Remove from the heat. Stir in the peanut butter. Taste and season with a little salt or sugar.

## variations:

**Smooth:** purée the soup with a stick blender until you have the texture you're after.

**Fragrant:** serve with a handful of Thai or regular basil leaves scattered over the top. Finely sliced fresh kaffir lime leaves are also a lovely addition.

**Nut-free:** replace the peanut butter with a little sugar and some fish sauce to season.

**Almond butter:** the first few times I made this soup I used some homemade almond butter which was just delicious.

**Carnivore:** simmer some finely sliced chicken breast or thigh fillets along with the broccoli.

**Other curry pastes:** while I think green curry works best with broccoli, feel free to use yellow, red or massaman instead.

# chickpea noodle soup

serves 2

- 2 cloves garlic, finely sliced
- 400g can chickpeas
- 95g soba noodles
- 2 tablespoons lemon juice
- 2 spring onions, sliced

There's something so special about soup with noodles. I think it's to do with the way you need a fork (or chopsticks) as well as a spoon. That and the wonderful slurping noises they encourage.

The first noodle soup I ever ate was good old chicken noodle out of a packet. When Mum was struggling with something for lunch, she'd pull out a sachet and the problem was solved. We all loved chasing noodles around the bowl.

This soup was inspired by the search for a vegetarian version of my childhood soup. To be honest, I like this version a whole lot more. The chickpeas bring a satisfying nutty element to it.

I've used the liquid from the chickpea can as the 'stock' for this soup. I was a little nervous about how it would taste, but was pleasantly surprised.

1. Heat some olive oil in a large saucepan and fry garlic over a medium-high heat until golden-brown, about 30 seconds.

2. Add chickpeas, their juices and 625ml water. Bring to the boil.

3. Add noodles. Simmer for 3 minutes until the noodles are almost cooked through.

4. Add lemon juice. Taste and season. Serve with spring onions sprinkled over.

## variations:

**Gluten-free:** replace the soba with rice noodles or other gluten-free noodles and adjust the cooking time according to the directions on the packet.

**No canning liquid/lower sodium:** if the thought of using the canning liquid from the chickpeas makes you feel a little funny, just skip it and increase the water to 750ml.

**Carnivore:** replace the water with chicken stock and either add a few handfuls of shredded cooked chicken or replace the chickpeas completely with the same weight of cooked chicken.

**Healthier:** some veg wouldn't go astray. Either add a handful or two of frozen peas in with the chickpeas or stir in a few handfuls of baby spinach after the noodles are cooked.

10-minute trick:

Boil the kettle before you start and use
this water when you add the chickpeas.

# fiery tomato and couscous soup

- 2 cloves garlic, finely chopped
- 1 teaspoon dried chilli flakes
- 400g can tomatoes, chopped
- 2 tablespoons soy sauce
- 95g couscous

Couscous is great in soups because it adds a hearty texture without being too stodgy.

If you aren't going to serve this straight away, either top up with a little water before serving, or wait until you're ready to serve before adding the couscous.

If the thought of a fiery soup excites you, you may want to increase the chilli. For those with delicate taste buds, feel free to dial down the fieriness or omit it all together.

1. Heat a few tablespoons olive oil in a large saucepan.

2. Fry garlic on a medium-high heat until starting to brown – about 30 seconds.

3. Add chilli, tomatoes, soy sauce and 375ml water and bring to the boil.

4. Simmer for about 5 minutes.

5. Add couscous and simmer for another few minutes until couscous is tender.

6. Taste, season and serve drizzled with a little extra virgin olive oil.

variations:

**Soy-free:** skip the soy sauce and replace the water with vegetable or chicken stock.

**Gluten-free:** replace the couscous with 150g of cooked brown rice or cooked quinoa and just bring back to a simmer.

**Short on time?** Skip the garlic.

**Carnivore:** replace the water with chicken stock and stir in a few handfuls of shredded cooked chicken with the couscous.

# 'healthy' green goddess soup

serves 2

- 1 bunch broccolini or 1 large head broccoli, chopped
- 2 small courgettes, finely chopped
- 4–6 tablespoons pesto

I read about a salad dressing made with mashed avocado in Alice Waters's *Chez Panisse: Vegetables*. While this soup has nothing to do with the salad, and certainly doesn't contain any avocado, it is so pretty and green that I felt it was worthy of the 'green goddess' title.

For me, the best commercial pestos are the ones in the chiller section of my favourite deli rather than in a jar.

1. Place broccolini or broccoli and courgettes in a medium saucepan with 625ml water.

2. Simmer for 6–7 minutes or until vegetables are tender.

3. Purée in a blender or using a stick blender until you have a smoothish soup.

4. Return to the heat. Stir through pesto.

5. Taste and season. Serve hot.

## variations:

**Vegan/dairy-free:** replace the pesto with basil oil (purée a bunch of basil with enough oil to make a paste) or make a Sicilian nut pesto by whizzing together 1 bunch basil, 1–2 cloves garlic, 1 cup cashews, 120ml extra virgin olive oil and a squeeze of lemon.

**Nut-free:** replace the pesto with basil oil as above or serve with loads of freshly grated parmesan.

**Carnivore:** grill some bacon or prosciutto till crisp and scatter over the soup.

**Cheesy:** replace the pesto with crumbled soft goat's cheese, or use cheese in addition to the pesto.

10-minute trick:

Boil the kettle before you start and use this
water to speed up the boiling process.

# easy japanese 'kettle' soup

serves 2

- large handful frozen peas
- 100g tofu
- 1 sheet nori, optional
- 1 heaped teaspoon dashi powder or stock
- 2 teaspoons soy sauce

Kettle soups are a brilliant solution when you don't have access to a proper kitchen but feel like a warm meal. All you need is some boiling water and a heatproof container, preferably with a lid.

If you haven't ever used dashi, an instant Japanese fish stock, I highly recommend giving it a go. You'll need to go to a large supermarket or an Asian grocery store to find it (and the nori sheet) but it will keep in the pantry for years. If that seems like too much trouble, just use a good-quality chicken or vegetable stock or bouillon powder.

1. Pop your kettle on to boil.

2. Place peas in a large heatproof container and cover with boiling water. Stand.

3. Slice tofu finely and tear nori, if using, into small squares.

4. Drain peas and return to your container, then add tofu, dashi and soy. Cover with fresh boiling water.

5. Stand for a minute before serving with the nori sheets, if using, on top.

## variations:

**Soy-free/carnivore:** replace the tofu with a handful of shredded cooked chicken and just use salt to season instead of the soy.

**Different veg:** replace the dashi with vegetable stock (bouillon) powder or use a tablespoon of white miso paste instead.

**More substantial:** increase the amount of tofu or add a handful of fresh udon noodles instead.

**Can't find nori?** Just skip it, or replace with a tablespoon of chopped chives or finely sliced spring onion.

# spiced lentil soup
## with yoghurt

serves 2

- 2 cloves garlic, finely sliced
- 1–2 teaspoons dried chilli flakes
- 4 teaspoons garam masala
- 2 x 400g cans lentils
- 4 tablespoons natural yoghurt, to serve

My love affair with canned lentils continues with this recipe. If you have a burning desire to cook dried lentils, that would be fine, especially if you have a stash of puy lentils. The canned lentils do a marvellous job though. Don't feel guilty about them. Earthy, hearty, a little bit healthy-feeling – you can't go wrong really.

1. Heat a few tablespoons olive oil in a medium saucepan.

2. Cook garlic over a high heat until browned – about 30 seconds.

3. Add chilli and garam masala and cook for another few seconds.

4. Add lentils and the liquid from the cans with an additional 125ml water.

5. Simmer for 7–8 minutes.

6. Taste and season. Serve with yoghurt.

## variations:

**Vegan/dairy-free:** replace the yoghurt with a mixture of 2 tablespoons tahini and 2 tablespoons lemon juice.

**Healthier:** stir in a few handfuls of frozen peas or baby spinach and simmer until warmed through or wilted.

**Short on time?** Skip the garlic.

**Higher protein/more substantial:** toss in some diced tofu or shredded chicken or cooked sliced pork sausages to warm through before serving.

**Can't find garam masala?** Replace with 2 teaspoons ground cumin and 2 teaspoons ground coriander, or try 4 teaspoons of your favourite curry powder.

# simple minestrone soup

serves 2

- 1 medium courgette, finely sliced into coins
- 2 cloves garlic, finely sliced
- 400g can tomatoes
- 400g can cannellini beans, or other white beans
- 4 tablespoons pesto, to serve

I love how the juices from the beans give this soup a dense, soupy texture. They also add a rich slow-cooked depth of flavour. You'll think your adopted Italian *nonna* has been simmering the soup for hours rather than the quick 5 minutes you've actually allowed.

1. Heat a few tablespoons olive oil in a large saucepan.

2. Cook courgette and garlic over a medium-high heat for a few minutes or until the courgette is starting to soften.

3. Add tomatoes, beans and the liquid from the cans. Simmer for another 5 minutes or until the courgette is cooked through.

4. Taste and season.

5. Serve hot with the pesto on top.

variations:

**Vegan/dairy-free:** replace the pesto with a handful of torn basil leaves or some basil oil and a handful of toasted pinenuts.

**Different veg:** replace the courgette with cavolo nero, cabbage or baby spinach.

**More substantial:** add a few handfuls of cooked short pasta such as penne or add a few handfuls of torn rustic sourdough or ciabatta – a great way to use up stale leftover bread.

**Tomato alternative:** replace the canned tomatoes with about 400ml tomato purée, passata or commercial tomato pasta sauce.

# udon noodle soup
## with spinach and tofu

- 200g tofu, preferably smoked, sliced into batons
- 400g 'fresh' udon noodles (see introduction)
- 4 tablespoons soy sauce
- 2 tablespoons lemon juice
- 3 large handfuls baby spinach

Udon noodles are the best for soup. Fat and slippery, they're also challenging to eat with chopsticks but don't let that stop you. You can get packaged udon that look fresh, but keep well in the pantry. They are great to have on hand for a last-minute meal.

1. Heat 2 tablespoons olive oil in a large saucepan over medium-high heat.

2. Add tofu and cook for about 2 minutes until golden.

3. Add 750ml boiling water. Bring back to the boil.

4. Add noodles and cook, stirring to separate for about 3 minutes.

5. Season with soy and lemon juice.

6. Add spinach and stir until wilted.

## variations:

**Carnivore/tofu-free:** if tofu isn't your thing, replace it with another source of protein like canned white beans or a handful of shredded cooked chicken.

**Soy-free:** skip the soy sauce and replace the water with vegetable or chicken stock.

**Different veg:** feel free to play around. Asian greens such as sliced bok choy or Chinese broccoli are lovely. Add them with the noodles as they will take a little longer to cook than the spinach.

**Gluten-free:** use rice or other gluten-free noodles; even gluten-free spaghetti will work. Just remember to adjust the cooking time according to the packet instructions.

10-minute trick:

Boil the kettle before you start and use this water to make the soup.

## 10-minute trick:

Boil the kettle before you start and use this water to cook the lentils. Make sure you keep the saucepan lid on to keep as much heat in as possible.

# hearty red lentil soup

serves 2

- 185g dried red lentils, rinsed
- ½–1 teaspoon dried chilli flakes
- 1 tablespoon ground cumin
- 400g can tomatoes, chopped
- natural yoghurt, to serve

There are few things more comforting than a big bowl of lentils or a warming bowl of soup. Combine the two and we're talking comfort central.

To keep this under 10 minutes, I've left the lentils a bit on the 'al dente' side. I quite like this chunky texture. If you'd prefer your soup to be more silky, cook the lentils a little longer and purée with a stick blender before serving.

1. Place lentils, chilli, cumin, tomatoes and 625ml water in a medium saucepan and bring to the boil.

2. Cover and boil for 9 minutes or until lentils are cooked to your liking.

3. Taste and season. Serve with a dollop of natural yoghurt.

## variations:

**Dairy-free:** skip the yoghurt and serve with a good drizzle of extra virgin olive oil. Coconut cream will also work here, but will completely change the flavour profile – not necessarily a bad thing!

**Different lentils:** feel free to use other lentils; puy lentils are a favourite but brown lentils are also lovely. You'll just need to simmer for longer: around 20 minutes.

**Healthier:** if you feel the need for some veg, add a handful of fresh or frozen peas or chopped broccoli with the lentils, or wilt in some baby spinach at the end.

**Short on time?** Replace the dried lentils with 2 x 400g cans of lentils and skip the water. Just bring it up to a simmer and it's good to serve.

# pea *and* almond soup

serves 2

- 1 large knob butter
- 4 tablespoons ground almonds
- 500g frozen peas
- 1 bunch mint, leaves picked
- squeeze of lemon juice

Frozen peas are such a life saver. This is a brilliant soup to have in your repertoire because if you have a packet of peas in the freezer you know dinner is less than 10 minutes away.

If you don't have ground almonds you could grind them yourself, try another type of nut or just stir in a few handfuls of grated parmesan at the end instead.

1. Heat butter in a large saucepan over a high heat.

2. Add almonds and stir-fry for about 30 seconds.

3. Add peas and 750ml boiling water.

4. Simmer for about 5 minutes or until peas are tender.

5. Add mint and purée with a stick blender until you have a lovely smooth soup.

6. Taste and season with salt, pepper and a generous squeeze of lemon.

variations:

**Dairy-free/vegan:** replace the butter with a few tablespoons olive oil.

**Nut-free:** skip the almonds and just serve with a very generous handful or 2 of finely grated parmesan.

**No mint?** It's lovely without, or try replacing with basil or flat-leaf parsley.

**More substantial:** toss in a drained can of chickpeas to simmer with the peas.

# smoky tomato soup

serves 2

- 400g can lentils, drained
- 1 teaspoon dried chilli flakes
- 400g can tomatoes
- 1 tablespoon smoked paprika
- 1 tablespoon natural yoghurt, to serve

My friend Heidi made this soup for her two adorable girls, Esme and Martha, who aren't at school yet. Apparently it was a big hit – who knew smoky lentils would be popular with the pre-school crowd? If you are cooking for children you might like to tone down the chilli.

Smoked paprika is one of the most magical ingredients. If you can't find it the soup will be OK without, but I highly recommend tracking some down. I use dried chilli flakes because they look prettier, but feel free to use chilli powder (about ½ teaspoon) or 1–2 finely sliced fresh chillies.

1. Place lentils, chilli, tomatoes, paprika and 625ml water in a medium saucepan and bring to the boil.

2. Cover and boil for 8 minutes or until lentils are cooked to your liking.

3. Taste and season. Serve with a dollop of natural yoghurt.

## variations:

**Healthier:** stir in a few handfuls of frozen peas or baby spinach and simmer until warmed through or wilted.

**Higher protein/more substantial:** toss in some diced tofu or shredded chicken or cooked sliced pork sausages to warm through before serving.

**Can't find smoked paprika?** Use regular paprika or skip it and call it 'tomato and lentil soup'.

# thai chicken and lime soup

- 400ml can coconut milk
- 2 tablespoons Thai green curry paste
- 3–4 chicken thigh fillets
- 6 kaffir lime leaves, finely sliced with scissors
- 1 bunch coriander, leaves picked

The Thai people sure know how to make a good soup – which always surprises me because their climate is so warm. Actually one of the best soups I ever ate was a chicken and noodle soup in a back alley in Bangkok on one of those sweltering days.

This soup is equally delicious on a chilly winter evening or a hot summer's day. The coconut creaminess makes it so warming in winter, but the fragrance of the coriander and lime leaves make it refreshing enough to serve when the weather is warmer.

1. Place a large saucepan over a high heat.

2. Scoop a tablespoon of the coconut cream from the top of the can and add it to the saucepan with the curry paste.

3. Cook for about 15 seconds and then add the rest of the coconut milk and 500ml water.

4. While it's coming to the boil, chop chicken into bite-sized pieces and add to the pot along with the lime leaves.

5. Simmer gently for 3–4 minutes or until the chicken is just cooked through.

6. Serve with coriander leaves.

## variations:

**Vegan/vegetarian:** replace the chicken with tofu or button mushrooms.

**Basil:** replace the fresh coriander with fresh basil or, better yet, fresh Thai basil.

**More substantial:** soften some rice noodles by covering in boiling water and leaving to stand while the chicken cooks. Drain and add to the soup before bringing back to the boil.

**Red soup:** just replace the green curry paste with red curry paste.

**No kaffir lime leaves?** Use the zest of a lime.

# salads

# shaved fennel salad *with* ricotta *and* warm peas

serves 2

- 2 tablespoons lemon juice
- 1 medium bulb fennel
- 100g frozen peas
- 200g ricotta
- small handful almonds, roughly chopped

I still remember being blown away by my first shaved fennel salad. The fresh aniseedy flavour and the wonderful crunchy texture were like discovering a whole new food planet. The secret to this salad is getting the fennel sliced as finely as possible. A mandoline makes the job easier, but a sharp knife and a steady hand will be fine. Don't stress if your fennel is a little thicker.

This salad is a meal in itself, but see 'variations' if you want it as an accompaniment to rich roast pork belly or even a classic roast chicken.

1. Mix lemon juice with 4 tablespoons extra virgin olive oil. Season.

2. Slice fennel crosswise as finely as possible, including any green fronds. Toss in the dressing.

3. Heat a tablespoon olive oil in a frying pan and cook peas over a medium heat for 5 minutes or until hot and sweet.

4. Smear ricotta on a serving platter or individual plates. Top with the fennel and scatter over peas and almonds.

## variations:

**Vegan/dairy-free:** replace the ricotta with hummus.

**Short on time?** Replace the frozen peas with a handful of mange tout and skip the whole warming thing.

**Side salad:** lose the ricotta and almonds for a less substantial salad that's lovely as a side to a bought roast or barbecue chicken or some Chinese barbecue pork.

**Nut-free:** just skip the almonds or replace with a handful of crunchy, toasted sourdough breadcrumbs.

# pea *and* lentil salad

serves 2

- 1 tablespoon sherry or white wine vinegar
- 400g can lentils, drained
- 2 handfuls frozen peas
- handful washed salad leaves
- parmesan

I love the contrasts in this salad: soft, earthy lentils with super-sweet, bright green peas. Don't feel that frozen peas are inferior. Unless you're growing your own and able to pick them straight from the garden, frozen peas will be much more flavoursome than anything in the shops.

If you have trouble tracking down canned lentils, feel free to cook your own. It will take a little longer but you should get them cooked in 20 minutes or so. Just simmer them in water like you would pasta – no need to soak or anything up front.

1. Bring your kettle to the boil.

2. Combine vinegar with 3 tablespoons extra virgin olive oil in a salad bowl. Season.

3. Toss drained lentils in the dressing.

4. Pour boiling water over the peas and drain.

5. Toss peas and leaves into the salad.

6. Serve with parmesan shaved over the top.

## variations:

**Carnivore:** toss in some finely sliced salami or prosciutto.

**Vegan/dairy-free:** skip the parmesan and serve the salad with sliced almonds instead.

**Different cheese:** a lovely creamy blue cheese would make a nice change from parmesan.

**Lentil-free:** for a lighter, fresher salad skip the lentils and double the amount of peas.

**No sherry vinegar?** Use lemon juice and toss in the zest of the lemon.

# green bean, dill and mustard salad

- 250g green beans, stalks trimmed
- 1 tablespoon white wine or sherry vinegar
- 2 tablespoons dijon mustard
- small handful dill
- small handful almonds, chopped

This salad makes a wonderful side dish to serve with roast chicken or fish. But you could also make a meal of it by adding some crusty bread, a poached egg, or even a drained can of chickpeas.

1. Bring a small saucepan of salted water to the boil.

2. Simmer beans for 5 minutes or until no longer crunchy.

3. Meanwhile, combine vinegar and mustard with 3 tablespoons extra virgin olive oil. Season.

4. Drain beans. Toss in the dressing while they are warm.

5. Add dill and almonds.

## variations:

**Mustard-free:** for a light dressing, just skip the mustard, but if you'd still like a creamy dressing, replace the olive oil with a good-quality whole-egg mayonnaise.

**No white wine or sherry vinegar?** Use lemon juice or rice-wine vinegar instead.

**No dill?** Replace with finely chopped flat-leaf parsley or mint.

**Nut-free:** skip the almonds or replace with ¼ of a small red onion, very finely diced.

10-minute trick:

Used boiled water from the kettle
to speed up the bean cooking.

# the classic mixed green salad

serves 2

- 1 tablespoon sherry vinegar
- ½ teaspoon soy sauce
- 3 handfuls mixed salad leaves, washed and dried

The most frequent thing I make is a simple green salad. It goes with pretty much anything and is a quick solution if you're like me and feel that a meal isn't complete without greens in some form. I've even convinced my Irishman that it's essential to have a green salad with our eggs for Sunday brunch.

My salad-dressing preferences go through phases. There's a complete list of my past favourite dressings on my Stonesoup blog. I thought I'd share my current favourite here. It's not my most minimalist dressing, but it does fall under 5 ingredients. Yay for salad!

1. Combine vinegar, soy sauce and 3 tablespoons extra virgin olive oil in a medium bowl.

2. Toss leaves gently in the dressing using clean hands.

3. Taste and season.

## variations:

No sherry vinegar? Rice-wine vinegar, lemon juice, red or white wine vinegar, champagne vinegar, even balsamic, would all work.

Soy-free: skip the soy sauce and be more generous with the salt, or try a dash of fish sauce instead.

Different leaves: pretty much anything you like – watercress, baby spinach, all lettuce, rocket, basil, parsley, mint, lovage, baby kale, baby cavolo nero or brussels sprout leaves.

Additional flavourings: sometimes I add a teaspoon of miso paste or a tablespoon of dijon or wholegrain mustard.

Other possibilities: shaved parmesan, goat's cheese, finely sliced ripe grapes, shaved pear, nuts and seeds.

# butter bean *and* smoked chicken salad

- 2 tablespoons lemon juice
- ¼ of a small red onion, finely diced
- 2 small handfuls shredded roast or smoked chicken
- 400g can butter beans, drained
- small bunch flat-leaf parsley, leaves picked

I love the complex flavour of smoked foods and smoked chicken is no exception: not only does it taste delicious, the smoking process helps it to last longer in the fridge, making it more convenient as well. That being said, this salad is also a great standby if you pick up a ready-roasted or barbecued chicken on the way home from work.

1. In a large bowl, whisk together lemon juice and 2 tablespoons extra virgin olive oil. Season.

2. Add onion, chicken, beans and parsley. Stir to combine.

3. Taste and season.

## variations:

**Vegan:** replace the chicken with 2 handfuls of roasted nuts – cashews are a favourite of mine. Or try a large handful of halved cherry tomatoes and a diced cucumber. Steamed broccoli florets would also be lovely.

**Vegetarian:** use crumbled goat's cheese or sliced hard-boiled eggs instead of the chicken.

**Carnivore:** replace chicken with a few slices of torn prosciutto.

**Leafy:** toss in a few handfuls of washed salad leaves as well as or instead of the parsley.

# soba noodle salad
## with tofu and lime

- 180g soba noodles
- 250g firm tofu, cut into batons
- 2 tablespoons lime juice + lime halves, to serve
- 2 tablespoons sesame oil
- 1 bunch coriander, leaves picked

Soba noodles are Japanese noodles made with buckwheat and they have a lovely nutty flavour. They're normally served cold with a dipping sauce, but I like to eat them both hot and cold.

I've been really getting into tofu since I spent a month being vegetarian. The secret is to buy the firmest tofu you can find – although if tofu isn't your thing, you could use chicken instead.

1. Cook noodles in boiling salted water for 4 minutes or until soft. Drain and cool under the cold tap.

2. Heat a few tablespoons olive oil in a frying pan. Cook tofu over a medium-high heat for a few minutes or until browned all over.

3. Combine lime juice and sesame oil in a large bowl.

4. Add noodles, tofu and coriander. Toss to combine.

## variations:

**Gluten-free:** use rice noodles or mung-bean (cellophane) noodles. Just cook according to the packet directions and refresh under cold running water, then proceed as per step 2.

**Carnivore:** chopped chicken breast or pork fillet would make a great alternative (or addition!) to the tofu. Just make sure it's cooked through.

**No coriander?** Replace with fresh mint or basil leaves.

**Can't find sesame oil?** Use olive oil and serve with toasted sesame seeds sprinkled over.

**Nut/sesame-free:** use olive oil instead.

# tomato, bread *and* bocconcini salad

- 375g small super-ripe tomatoes, halved
- 1 tablespoon sherry or white wine vinegar
- 1 large chunk rustic bread (about 100g), crust removed and torn into chunks
- 2–3 sprigs flat-leaf parsley, leaves picked
- small handful baby bocconcini or buffalo mozzarella, torn

This is a combination of two Italian salads: 'panzanella', a fresh tomato and bread salad, and 'insalata Caprese', a minimalist combination of buffalo mozzarella, ripe tomato and basil. The result is a wonderfully satisfying salad, a perfect summer meal in itself. You could serve it as a more substantial side salad with a roast chicken or some grilled sausages.

Bread salads are a great way to use up stale bread, but fresh is also fine. If you're after a vegan version, this salad is also lovely as a simple tomato and bread salad.

1. Squash tomatoes a little to release some of their juice.

2. Combine vinegar and 3 tablespoons extra virgin olive oil. Season.

3. Add dressing to the tomatoes, along with the bread, parsley and cheese.

4. Gently toss. Taste and season.

## variations:

**Vegan/dairy-free:** replace the cheese with extra bread and a good drizzle of olive oil, or throw in a handful of roasted almonds.

**Gluten-free:** replace the bread with a drained can of butter beans or chickpeas.

**Different herbs:** basil is a more usual partner to tomatoes.

**Budget:** replace bocconcini with a cheaper cheese like ricotta.

# black quinoa *and* broccolini salad

serves 2

- 100g black quinoa
- 1 bunch broccolini, chopped
- 1 tablespoon balsamic vinegar
- small bunch chives, finely chopped
- handful whole almonds, toasted

To be honest, I don't find a massive difference in the flavour of the different colours of quinoa, so if you can only find white or red, go ahead and use that. In keeping with my 10 minutes' time limit, the quinoa comes out on the more 'al dente' side, which I quite like. If you prefer your grains softer and more tender, just cook a few minutes longer.

This salad is equally lovely when freshly made or when it's been in the fridge for a day or so. A great thing to make for work or school lunches

1. Bring a medium saucepan of salted water to the boil.

2. Cook quinoa for 5 minutes. Add broccolini and continue cooking for another 4 minutes.

3. Meanwhile mix balsamic vinegar with 3 tablespoons extra virgin olive oil. Season.

4. Drain broccolini and quinoa and toss in the dressing.

5. Add chives and almonds and serve hot, warm or chilled.

## variations:

**Carnivores:** serve as a side dish to a steak or roast leg of lamb. Or replace the almonds with a few rashers of bacon that have been fried until crisp.

**Nut-free:** replace the almonds with some torn buffalo mozzarella, slices of goat's cheese, a few chunks of ricotta or some generous shavings of parmesan.

**Can't find quinoa?** Replace with 180g of cooked grains such as brown rice, or try a drained can of chickpeas or butter beans. If using this option you can just cook the broccolini on its own.

**No broccolini?** Regular broccoli will be equally delicious, or try Chinese broccoli, broccoli rabe, purple-sprouting broccoli or even green asparagus.

# triple 'c' salad

- 2 tablespoons lemon juice
- ½ teaspoon cumin seeds
- 2 medium carrots
- 3 sprigs parsley, leaves picked
- large handful cashews, roasted

Carrot, cumin and cashews: the holy trinity of the triple 'C' salad. If only I'd thought about it before I added the parsley – just a little coriander or chives would have made a quadruple C!

It's easy to forget about how delicious carrots can be. This salad shows them in all their crunchy vibrant goodness. It's anything but boring.

1. Combine lemon juice with cumin seeds and 3 tablespoons extra virgin olive oil in a large bowl. Season with salt and pepper.

2. Grate or shred carrots using a grater or food processor and add to the dressing.

3. Add parsley. Toss, taste and season.

4. Serve with cashews sprinkled over.

## variations:

**Carnivore:** toss in a little crispy bacon instead of the cashews.

**Nut-free:** replace the cashews with a few tablespoons finely chopped red onion or handful of toasted breadcrumbs.

**Creamy:** replace the olive oil with good-quality mayonnaise.

**More substantial:** increase the amount of cashews or replace the nuts with shredded barbecue chicken or hard-boiled eggs.

**Colourful:** if you come across some purple carrots, use these instead of or as well as the orange carrots. Or try some raw beetroot in the salad as well.

salads 73

**10-minute trick:**

Much quicker to grate the carrot using a food processor but it does make for more washing up at the end!

# chickpea *and* parmesan salad

- 1 tablespoon lemon juice
- 400g can chickpeas, drained
- handful mixed salad leaves, washed
- small handful grated parmesan

The tricky thing with this salad is that a whole tin of chickpeas can be quite a big eat. If you're not super hungry, feel free to ditch some of the chickpeas and save them for another meal. Or just use a small can of chickpeas.

If I'm in the mood for a little spice I sometimes add a pinch of ground cumin or some dried chilli. But usually I eat it as is. If you don't have any salad leaves on hand, a few fresh parsley leaves work well or you could just skip the greenery altogether.

1. Mix lemon juice with 1 tablespoon extra virgin olive oil in a small bowl.

2. Season generously.

3. Toss chickpeas and salad in the dressing.

4. Grate over parmesan and serve.

variations:

**Vegan/dairy-free:** just skip the parmesan or replace it with finely grated brazil nuts or flaked almonds.

**Carnivores:** a few slices of prosciutto or jamón, torn and tossed in with the cheese, wouldn't go astray.

**No leaves?** If there isn't anything fresh in the house and I'm looking for a meal from the pantry, I skip the greenery and just make it with chickpeas, parmesan and a little vinegar.

**Different cheese:** parmesan is a favourite because it keeps for ages in the fridge, but this is also lovely with a soft goat's cheese or crumbled salty feta.

# brown rice salad

serves 2

- 2 tablespoons lemon juice
- 180g cooked brown rice, chilled
- ¼ of a small red onion, finely chopped
- small bunch flat-leaf parsley, leaves chopped
- small bunch mint, leaves picked

This salad is a permanent staple in my house. It's wonderfully versatile, but this version is the simplest. And if the truth be told, it's also my favourite.

If I'm in a hurry I use pre-cooked rice from the supermarket. But it's also great to have a stash of cooked brown rice in the freezer that you can quickly defrost. It can be made ahead and refrigerated until needed, which makes it ideal both for entertaining and for packed lunches.

1. Combine lemon juice with 4 tablespoons extra virgin olive oil. Season.

2. Add rice, onion, parsley and mint and toss to combine.

3. Taste and season.

## variations:

**Carnivores:** stir through some cooked chicken. It's also a great side salad to serve with roast beef or lamb or anywhere you'd normally serve tabbouleh.

**More substantial:** to make it more of a meal on its own, toss in some roasted nuts, hard-boiled eggs, cooked chicken or canned tuna.

**Different grains:** this is lovely with cooked quinoa, barley or lentils instead of the rice.

**Different herbs:** you could use either parsley or mint on their own, or substitute some fresh coriander leaves, lovage or basil for one or the other.

**Milder:** either skip the red onion altogether or use a small handful of chopped chives instead.

# thai-inspired beef salad

serves 2

- 3 tablespoons lime juice + zest
- 3 tablespoons fish sauce
- 2 cucumbers
- 200g rare roast beef
- 1 bunch mint, leaves picked

I tend to make this salad just in summer but sometimes it sneaks into the cooler months as a warm salad. If that appeals, either stir-fry some finely sliced beef fillet or toss the deli beef in a hot pan for a few minutes.

1. Combine the lime zest, juice, fish sauce and 3 tablespoons peanut oil in a medium-sized bowl.

2. Halve cucumbers lengthwise and chop into little half-moons. Add to the dressing.

3. Tear the beef into bite-sized pieces and add to the dressing.

4. Add mint leaves and toss gently.

## variations:

**Vegan/vegetarian:** a Thai mushroom salad would be lovely. Just replace the beef with finely sliced roasted or pan-fried field mushrooms and use soy sauce instead of the fish sauce.

**Fish-free:** replace the fish sauce with soy sauce.

**Cucumber-free:** use sliced green peppers or a few handfuls of well-washed beansprouts in place of the cucumber.

**Hot!** Add a few finely sliced small red chillies to the dressing.

**Different herbs:** fresh coriander, basil or Thai basil would all work in addition to or instead of the mint.

# quinoa *and* parsley salad *with* almonds

serve 2

- 90g quinoa
- 2 tablespoons lemon juice
- 1 teaspoon ground cumin
- 1 bunch flat-leaf parsley, stems finely chopped, leaves coarsely chopped
- handful whole almonds

Quinoa is one of my favourite grains at the moment. It has a unique chewy texture – a little like pearl barley – and a wonderfully wholesome flavour. If you can't find quinoa, this salad is also lovely with any other cooked grains. Barley would be great or even couscous.

I'm happy to eat this as a meal on its own, but it also goes really well with pita bread and some hummus.

1. Bring a medium saucepan of salted water to the boil.

2. Cook quinoa for 9 minutes or until tender.

3. Meanwhile mix lemon juice, cumin and 4 tablespoons extra virgin olive oil in a large bowl. Season.

4. Drain quinoa and stir into the lemon mixture.

5. Toss in parsley and almonds.

6. Taste and season.

## variations:

**Nut-free:** just skip the almonds or replace with a little finely chopped red onion or a handful of crunchy pan-fried breadcrumbs.

**Can't find quinoa?** Try other grains or legumes such as barley, brown rice or red lentils, but they'll take longer to cook. Or soak 95g couscous in 125ml boiling water for 5 minutes before fluffing with a fork and tossing in the dressing.

**Different greens:** try fresh mint or basil or salad leaves. Finely sliced kale or cavolo nero also work really well.

**More substantial:** increase the nuts or serve with boiled or poached eggs or some cooked chicken or canned tuna.

# salmon *and* mixed leaf salad

- 180g can salmon, drained
- 1 bag washed salad leaves
- 1 lemon

This is my go-to lunch whether I'm out and about or just at home alone. Just pop into the supermarket and pick up a bag of washed leaves, a can of fish and a lemon.

1. Mash salmon with a fork to break up any tiny bones.

2. Open salad bag and add the salmon.

3. Squeeze over a little lemon juice and eat with a fork out of the bag.

variations:

**Vegan:** replace the salmon with canned or cooked chickpeas or mushrooms.

**Vegetarian:** try some cheese such as a goat's cheese or ricotta instead of the salmon. Hard-boiled eggs are also great.

**Different leaves:** any salad leaves are good, especially baby spinach or finely shredded kale. Super-finely sliced cabbage is also really lovely.

**Different fish:** any canned fish is good, especially tuna or sardines. For a fancier option try smoked salmon.

# shredded kale *and* white bean salad

- 2 tablespoons sherry vinegar
- 1 tablespoon soy sauce
- 1 bunch kale or other greens
- 400g can cannellini beans, drained
- 1 small onion or shallot, finely chopped and fried, optional

When I was recently in the US I had a wonderful time exploring my local Whole Foods, particularly their amazing salad bar. One of the best was kale with cannellini beans, two of my all-time favourite foods together at last!

1. Combine sherry vinegar and soy with 3 tablespoons extra virgin olive oil in a large bowl. Season with salt and pepper.

2. Slice greens as finely as possible across the stem (removing the stem if it looks too thick).

3. Toss greens and beans in the dressing. Taste and season more if needed.

4. Arrange salad on a platter and serve with the onion scattered over, if using.

variations:

**Carnivore:** kale and bacon are wonderful friends, so feel free to crumble some crispy bacon over the top in place of the fried onions.

**No fried onions?** Replace with a little shaved parmesan or crumbled goat's cheese.

**Different beans:** if cannellini beans aren't your thing, try butter beans, red kidney or black-eye beans.

**Greens:** any dark leafy greens will work. Try cavolo nero, curly kale, collard greens, chard, spinach or even baby spinach.

# BBQ chicken *and* bread salad

serves 2

- 1 tablespoon sherry or red wine vinegar
- 1 tablespoon wholegrain mustard
- ½ a barbecued chicken
- 2 slices rustic bread, preferably sourdough, crust removed and torn into chunks
- 2 handfuls mixed salad leaves

This is one of my all-time favourite one-bowl meals. It couldn't be easier. Here I've used a barbecued chicken from the local takeaway. It's fast, delicious and feels like you've gone to a lot more effort than you actually have. If you have more time, feel free to roast your own chicken, and for something a little more exotic, try a barbecued duck from Chinatown.

1. Mix vinegar, mustard and 3 tablespoons extra virgin olive oil. Season.

2. Shred chicken meat, discarding bones. I like to keep the skin on, but it's up to you.

3. Toss chicken and bread in the dressing, pushing down so the bread soaks up the dressing.

4. Gently mix in salad leaves.

5. Taste and season.

variations:

**Gluten-free:** use gluten-free bread, 160g of cooked brown rice or quinoa, a handful of roasted nuts, or – my favourite – a drained can of butter or cannellini beans.

**Vegetarian/vegan:** replace chicken with 2 large portobello or field mushrooms that have been roasted until tender (about 30 minutes at 180°C). Or just replace the chicken with a generous handful of roast almonds or cashews.

**Crunchy:** toss in a handful of roasted pinenuts or almonds.

**Asian-vibe:** replace the chicken with roast or barbecue duck and use rice vinegar and soy sauce to replace the vinegar and mustard.

# super light coleslaw with chicken

serves 2

- 4 tablespoons whole-egg mayonnaise
- 2 tablespoons lemon juice
- ¼ of a white cabbage
- 3 sprigs flat-leaf parsley, leaves picked
- 160g smoked chicken, optional

Growing up, I didn't ever 'get' coleslaw. I think it was the gloopy mayonnaise and lurid colours from the carrots and red cabbage. When I started getting into shaved cabbage salads, it was a simple step to adding a little mayo to the dressing. And now I love my 'slaw.

I've served this salad with some smoked chicken tossed through, but you could easily use a store-bought BBQ chicken or just serve it on its own. A handful of roasted almonds is good for a little more crunch.

This is one of those wonderfully low-maintenance salads that will sit happily in the fridge for a few hours or even days until you're ready to eat it. Although best to stir in the parsley at the last moment to avoid it wilting.

1. Combine mayonnaise and lemon juice in a large bowl. Season with salt and pepper.

2. Remove tough core from the cabbage then finely shred using a sharp knife and a steady hand or a mandoline.

3. Toss cabbage in the mayonnaise mixture along with the parsley.

4. Shred chicken if using, and toss into the salad.

variations:

**Vegan/egg-free:** use vegan mayonnaise or just extra virgin olive oil, and replace the chicken with a drained can of white beans.

**Vegetarian:** replace chicken with a couple of hard-boiled eggs.

**Colourful:** play around with red or other cabbage. A handful of grated carrot is also lovely.

**Courgette slaw:** replace cabbage with 2–3 courgettes, finely shaved into ribbons with a vegetable peeler or a mandoline.

**Spring slaw:** replace the parsley with a small bunch of asparagus, shaved into ribbons with a vegetable peeler.

# raw broccoli salad

serves 2

- 1 tablespoon wholegrain mustard
- 1 tablespoon sherry vinegar
- 1 head broccoli
- 1 avocado
- handful roasted almonds

I just adore the way the avocado and broccoli combine in this salad to give crunch and creamy richness. I think I've discovered a new food marriage made in heaven.

1. Combine mustard, vinegar and 3 tablespoons extra virgin olive oil in a salad bowl. Season.

2. Chop broccoli into tiny trees and toss in the dressing.

3. Chop avocado in half and scoop bite-sized chunks into the dressing using a spoon.

4. Toss salad to distribute the dressing and serve with almonds on top.

variations:

**Carnivore:** replace the avocado with a few handfuls of fried crispy bacon.

**Nut-free:** replace the almonds with sesame seeds or finely diced red pepper or red onion.

**Herby:** serve sprinkled with fresh herbs such as coriander, parsley, mint or basil.

**More substantial:** add a few more almonds or serve with some shredded poached chicken or some prosciutto; canned tuna or salmon would also be lovely. Vegetarians could toss in a drained can of chickpeas or white beans.

# blue cheese *and* walnut salad

- 1 tablespoon sherry vinegar
- 1 small head radicchio
- small bunch flat-leaf parsley, leaves picked
- 150g creamy blue cheese
- handful of walnuts

This salad was inspired by a wonderful dish I had recently at the iconic Bistro Moncur in Sydney. There's something about well-dressed leaves contrasting creamy cheese and crunchy nuts that just works so well together.

Feel free to play around with the cheese/nut/leaves combo. A soft goat's cheese with baby spinach and roasted almonds would be a great place to start.

1. Combine vinegar with 4 tablespoons extra virgin olive oil in a large salad bowl. Season.

2. Tear radicchio leaves into chunky pieces. Wash and spin dry. You may not want to use all the radicchio.

3. Toss leaves into the dressing along with the parsley leaves.

4. Arrange leaves on a platter or in a bowl.

5. Break cheese into chunks and scatter over the leaves.

6. Top with walnuts.

## variations:

**Different cheese:** replace the blue cheese with whatever takes your fancy. A fresh young goat's cheese would be lovely, as would generous lashings of shaved parmesan.

**Carnivore:** serve with crispy bacon or finely sliced prosciutto.

**Vegan/dairy-free:** replace cheese with scoops of avocado flesh.

**Fruit:** some finely sliced pear would be a nice addition for both the sweetness and the crunch.

# white bean *and* avocado salad

serves 2

- 2 tablespoons lemon juice
- 400g can white beans, drained
- 4 handfuls baby spinach
- 1 avocado
- small handful roasted almonds

I just adore avocado in salads. Creamy and filling, it's perfect against leafy greens with a sharp dressing.

To turn it into more of a main course, dinner-time salad, I've taken to adding canned white beans. The beans soak up the dressing and make for a more substantial-feeling salad without being OTT.

While it works completely as a main course salad, you could also serve as a side salad.

1. Combine lemon juice with 3 tablespoons extra virgin olive oil in a large salad bowl. Season generously.

2. Toss drained beans and baby spinach in the dressing.

3. Halve avocado, scoop out bite-sized pieces of flesh with a spoon and add to the salad.

4. Divide salad between two plates and serve with almonds sprinkled over.

variations:

**Carnivore:** avocado and bacon are great friends, so replace the almonds with some crispy fried bacon pieces. Add a few halved tomatoes for a classic BLT salad.

**No baby spinach?** Just use whichever mixed salad leaves you have on hand.

**Nut-free:** replace the almonds with some halved cherry tomatoes for colour or some finely diced red onion or red pepper for crunch.

**Mexican salad:** replace lemon juice with lime and toss in a little dried or fresh chilli to spice things up.

# shaved courgette salad

serves 2

- 2 tablespoons lemon juice
- 2 medium courgettes
- small handful flat-leaf parsley leaves

This is one of my favourite salads at the moment. I just love the crunchy texture of courgettes. It's a super-versatile salad because the courgette doesn't go soggy as it marinates in the dressing, so it's brilliant to make ahead.

Turn it into a meal on its own with a generous handful of roasted nuts and some cooked or canned lentils or chickpeas.

1. Combine lemon juice with 2 tablespoons extra virgin olive oil in a medium bowl. Season.

2. Using a vegetable peeler, a mandoline or a sharp knife and a steady hand, shave the courgettes into very fine ribbons.

3. Toss courgettes in the dressing with the parsley.

variations:

**Carnivore:** lovely with some finely sliced prosciutto draped over the top.

**Herby:** play around with the herbs – mint, basil or chives are all good.

**Asian-inspired:** replace the parsley with coriander leaves and the lemon juice with lime juice. A splash of fish sauce is also lovely instead of salt to season.

# vegetables

# big plate of greens with parmesan

serves 4

- 1 clove garlic, finely sliced
- 1 large bunch cavolo nero, coarsely chopped
- 2 tablespoons lemon juice
- small handful shaved parmesan

This is my favourite single-gal meal. When I'm cooking for myself and I want something quick and healthy, it's hard to go past a big plate of greens.

Sometimes I spice things up with a small handful of toasted pinenuts or almonds, but mostly I enjoy the greens on their own with a little garlic, a squeeze of lemon and some parmesan shavings. Oh, and a massive pot of lemongrass and ginger tea.

1. Heat a few tablespoons of olive oil in a large frying pan.

2. Cook garlic over a medium-high heat for about 30 seconds or until starting to brown.

3. Add greens and continue to cook, stirring for a few minutes, until they are just wilted.

4. Remove from the heat. Taste and season with salt, pepper and a little lemon juice.

5. Serve hot with shaved parmesan.

## variations:

**Dairy-free/vegan:** replace the parmesan with pinenuts or almonds.

**Carnivore:** serve as a side dish to a roast leg of lamb, or with finely sliced prosciutto scattered over the top.

**Different greens:** spinach, chard, collard greens or Chinese broccoli are all lovely; another favourite is the inky greenness of curly kale.

**Higher protein:** fried or poached egg can be a lovely accompaniment, or toss in a drained can of beans or lentils to heat through at the end.

**Different cheese:** lovely with a sharp goat's cheese or a piquant blue crumbled over.

This is all about getting the mushies cooked. So before you even
think about doing anything, get your pan on a super high heat.

# mushroom 'steaks'

serves 2

- 4 large portobello or field mushrooms
- 1 clove garlic, very finely chopped
- small bunch thyme, leaves picked
- 4–6 tablespoons mayonnaise
- 2 large handfuls baby spinach

If you're ever in need of something meaty and vegetarian, it's hard to beat a good mushroom 'steak'.

By searing portobello or field mushies in a hot pan, in much the same way you'd cook a steak, you get wonderfully concentrated mushrooms in a fraction of the time it would take to roast them. I love how the juices leak out and sear, making a super savoury crust on the outside of each mushie.

1. Heat a large frying pan on a very high heat.

2. Trim mushroom stalks and add to the pan with a little olive oil. Sear mushrooms for about 8 minutes, turning every 2 minutes.

3. Meanwhile, finely chop garlic and stir with the thyme into the mayo.

4. Serve mushies with a good dose of salt and pepper and with mayo and leaves on the side.

## variations:

**Carnivore:** serve with some finely sliced prosciutto draped over the top.

**Vegan/egg-free:** use vegan mayo, or replace with hummus or a tahini-based sauce.

**Higher protein:** beef it up by stirring one or two hard-boiled eggs in with the mayo.

**Cheesy mushrooms:** skip the mayo and cook the mushies for 4 minutes, gill-side down, then turn and grate some cheese over the top to melt while they finish cooking. If the cheese isn't melted enough for you, pop under a hot grill for a little while.

**Barbecue mushies:** rub with a little oil and barbecue on a high heat just as you would for a steak. They'll take 3–4 minutes each side depending on size.

# aubergine *with* chickpeas

- 1 large aubergine, diced into 1½cm cubes
- 400g can chickpeas, drained
- 2 teaspoons ground coriander
- 1–2 tablespoons lemon juice
- small bunch fresh coriander, leaves picked

While soft, silky aubergine is a thing of beauty, under-cooked aubergine is one of the worst things you can put in your mouth. The first time I made this I was a little nervous about getting the aubergine cooked within 10 minutes, but to my surprise it was a cinch. Covering the frying pan to keep the heat in and cutting the aubergine into relatively small chunks are the secrets to speedy cooking.

And don't worry about not salting the aubergine first: modern varieties don't have the bitterness that salting used to get rid of.

1. Heat a generous amount of olive oil in a large frying pan.

2. Cook aubergine chunks over a medium-high heat, covered. Stir every few minutes until aubergine is super soft and a little golden.

3. Add chickpeas and ground coriander and stir through until chickpeas are warm.

4. Remove from the heat and add 1 tablespoon lemon juice.

5. Taste and season, using extra lemon juice if you think it needs it.

6. Scatter over coriander leaves.

variations:

**Short on time?** Use grilled aubergine slices from the deli and just cook until everything is warm.

**Different legumes:** replace chickpeas with about 250g canned or home-cooked beans, lentils or quinoa.

**Herby:** mint, parsley or basil are good instead of the coriander.

**Cheesy:** it's lovely with goat's cheese or feta crumbled over.

10-minute trick:

Make sure you get the pan on to heat before you even think about chopping the broccoli. You want it smoking hot!

# super simple broccoli
## with almonds

serves 1

- 1 head broccoli
- small handful almonds
- small knob of butter
- squeeze of lemon juice

The basic idea behind this recipe comes from Heston Blumenthal, a chef who tends to be about as far from minimalist as possible. Who would have thought he'd come up with such a brilliant way to cook broccoli?

This is great as a meal on its own when you're in need of a serious veggie fix.

1. Heat a wok or large frying pan with a lid, until smoking hot.

2. Cut broccoli into little trees and finely slice the leftover stems.

3. Add 1 tablespoon extra virgin olive oil and broccoli to the pan. Jam on the lid.

4. Cook for 2 minutes. Stir and add butter and almonds.

5. Cover and cook for another 2 minutes or until broccoli is charred in places and tender and a little crunchy in others.

6. Squeeze over a little lemon juice. Taste and season.

## variations:

**Nut-free:** leave them out or replace with a small drained can of chickpeas.

**Carnivore:** pan-fry some bacon or minced beef and toss in at the end.

**Vegan/dairy-free:** replace butter with extra virgin olive oil.

**Leafy:** to make more of a salad, toss through any salad greens.

**More substantial:** toss in a drained can of chickpeas or serve with some hummus. Or toss with hot pasta and your best-quality extra virgin olive oil. Or add a drained can of tuna in oil, allow to warm through and serve with a wedge of lemon. Or team with a fried egg.

# mushies *with* butter beans

- 2 large field mushrooms (approx. 250g), halved and sliced
- 1 clove garlic, finely sliced
- 400g can butter beans, drained
- 1 tablespoon sherry or red wine vinegar
- 3 sprigs parsley, finely chopped

While pan-fried mushrooms on toast is an old favourite for a quick meal, this version with butter beans is a little more hearty and filling and possibly more delicious.

A very sparing drop or two of truffle oil would take it to another level, as would a couple of porcini mushrooms, soaked and chopped. But please don't feel like you need to go there.

1. Heat 3 tablespoons olive oil in a large frying pan.

2. Cook mushrooms and garlic over a medium-high heat. Stir frequently for about 8 minutes or until mushrooms are soft and a little browned.

3. Stir in the beans and allow to warm.

4. Remove from the heat and add vinegar. Taste and season.

5. Toss in the parsley and you're done.

## variations:

**Different mushrooms:** pretty much any mushroom will work here. Try portobello, wild mushrooms, oyster, shitake or a mixture.

**Short on time?** Nowhere near as tasty, but you could use canned mushrooms or champignons instead, and just cook until hot.

**Richer:** replace the olive oil with butter.

**Cheesy:** I love mushrooms and cheese, and this is wonderful with finely grated parmesan or ricotta or even some really crumbly aged cheddar.

# quick veg curry

- 400g jar tomato pasta sauce, e.g. napoletana or arrabbiata
- 400g can cannellini beans, drained
- 280g jar roasted red peppers, drained
- ½–1 teaspoon chilli flakes
- 4 teaspoons curry powder

While I just adore Indian food and restaurants, sometimes it's much nicer to make your own curry so you know exactly what has gone into it.

Choose your favourite curry powder here and be prepared to play around with the level. Likewise with the chilli. The veg are also something to adjust according to what you have on hand, although I love the simplicity of this version, using ingredients from my pantry.

1. Place tomato sauce, beans, peppers, chilli and curry powder in a pan and bring to a simmer.

2. Cook gently for 2–3 minutes or until the curry is hot.

3. Taste and season, adding more curry powder and chilli if you think it needs it. Serve with a generous drizzle of extra virgin olive oil.

variations:

**Carnivore:** brown some diced chicken, beef or pork in a pan then add the curry ingredients as per the recipe.

**Different veg:** feel free to add any veg you have on hand. Wilting some spinach or chard through will add a different dimension.

**No chilli flakes?** Use fresh chilli or chilli powder.

**No curry powder?** Replace with another spice blend such as garam masala or just use 2 teaspoons each of ground cumin and ground coriander.

**No tomato sauce?** Replace with canned tomatoes or tomato passata.

# steamed broccolini
## with lemon zest

- 1 head broccolini
- zest and juice of
  ½ a lemon

After a green salad, this is my second most commonly called-upon side dish. Bursting with freshness like a new spring day, it's a big dose of vitamins in a bowl. You won't be able to help feeling healthy and full of vitality after a bowl of these greens.

1. Place about 1cm water in the base of a medium saucepan. Cover and bring to the boil on a high heat.

2. Meanwhile, trim about 2cm off the bottom of the broccolini.

3. Add broccolini to the water and cook, covered, for 4–5 minutes or until broccolini is bright green and tender when pierced with a knife.

4. Drain broccolini if there's any water left and place in a serving dish.

5. Sprinkle over lemon zest and a squeeze of lemon and finish with a little salt and pepper and a drizzle of extra virgin olive oil.

variations:

**Carnivore:** serve with some finely sliced prosciutto.

**More substantial:** turn this into a meal by tossing in a drained can of white beans or cooked lentils, and be a little more generous with the olive oil and lemon juice.

**Different veg:** try regular, purple-sprouting or Chinese broccoli or even green asparagus.

**Chilli:** toss in a little fresh or dried chilli for a warming surprise.

10-minute trick:

Depending on your stove it may be quicker to use boiled water from the kettle.

10-minute trick:

Use a mandoline to shave the cabbage more quickly. And if you're really pressed for time, skip the bean cooking and garlic and serve the salad with beans at room temperature.

# shaved cabbage
## with white beans

serves 2

- 1 clove garlic, finely sliced
- 400g can white beans, drained
- ¼ of a white cabbage, very finely sliced
- 2 tablespoons lemon juice
- large handful finely grated parmesan

Shaved cabbage salad with parmesan and lemon juice has been on high rotation as a side salad at our place for a while now. But I wanted to make it into something more substantial, something warm and comforting to have on a winter's evening. This warm salad with white beans is the result.

1. Heat a few tablespoons olive oil in a large frying pan over a medium-high heat.

2. Add garlic and beans. Cook for a few minutes until garlic is browned and the beans are warm and starting to go a bit toasty on the outside.

3. Remove from the heat and toss in a bowl with the cabbage, lemon juice and parmesan.

4. Taste and season. Serve warm.

## variations:

**Different beans:** try pretty much any canned or cooked legume – butter beans, borlotti and chickpeas are all favourites of mine.

**Carnivore:** toss in some prosciutto or pancetta; smoked salmon is also lovely.

**Dairy-free/vegan:** replace the parmesan with finely grated brazil nuts.

**Fun:** toss in a few sprigs of parsley or mint for extra colour.

# red curry of potato and cashews

- 3–4 tablespoons red curry paste
- 400ml can coconut cream
- 750g can potatoes, drained
- 225g cashews, roasted
- small bunch basil, leaves picked

Along with chicken and cashew nuts, red curry was one of the first Thai dishes I learned to cook. I remember how time-consuming it was gathering all the ingredients and then pounding them to make a curry paste. These days I find commercial curry pastes are so good it's just not worthwhile making your own unless it's a very special occasion, or you're cooking for someone like my lovely Thai friend Jan.

And if you're worried about using canned potatoes, my Irishman loves this curry. Normally he would turn his nose up at the thought of anything other than fresh spuds, so don't feel bad about using canned here.

1. Heat a few tablespoons peanut or other vegetable oil in a wok over a high heat.

2. Add curry paste and stir-fry until fragrant – about 30 seconds.

3. Add coconut cream, potatoes and cashews. Bring to the boil.

4. Simmer for 5 minutes or until the sauce has thickened slightly and everything is hot.

5. Taste and season. You might like to add a little brown sugar.

6. Serve with basil scattered over.

## variations:

**Nut-free:** either remove the cashews or replace with a similar quantity of cooked chicken or tofu.

**Vegan/fish-free:** the Thai curry paste that I use (Ayam) doesn't contain fish sauce or shrimp paste, but many do, so check the ingredient list.

**Carnivores:** add some cooked strips of chicken, beef or even prawns.

**Fragrant:** use Thai basil if you can find it, or throw in a few kaffir lime leaves with the coconut cream.

10-minute trick:

To get the cauli cooked in time be sure to chop into very small trees. And get the pan on to heat while you're chopping the veg.

# cauliflower with smoked chicken

- ½ a head cauliflower, cut into tiny trees
- 1 tablespoon dijon mustard
- 1 tablespoon sherry vinegar
- 2 handfuls smoked chicken
- small bunch flat-leaf parsley, leaves picked

A great vegetable-focused dinner when you still feel like a bit of meat as well. The cauliflower needs to be cut into tiny trees – about the size of a grape – so it cooks in no time at all.

1. Heat a few tablespoons olive oil in a large wok or pan with a lid on a medium-high heat.

2. Cook cauliflower, covered, for about 8 minutes, stirring occasionally. If it starts to burn, add a few tablespoons water.

3. Meanwhile, mix mustard, vinegar and 1 tablespoon extra virgin olive oil. Season.

4. Add chicken to cauliflower and cook for another minute or until chicken is hot.

5. Remove from the heat and toss cauliflower and chicken in the dressing with the parsley.

variations:

**Vegan:** replace the chicken with smoked or regular almonds.

**Vegetarian:** skip the chicken and grate or crumble over your favourite cheese at the end. I love a good aged cheddar or parmesan.

**Short on time?** Serve the cauli raw, very finely sliced, tossed in the dressing.

**No sherry vinegar?** Try lemon juice or other wine vinegars such as white wine or champagne.

# vegetable *and* white bean stew

serves 3–4

- 2 x 400g cans white beans
- 2 x 400g cans tomatoes
- 2–3 courgettes, sliced into coins
- 2 tablespoons smoked paprika
- 2 large handfuls baby spinach

When you're in the mood for a serious veggie fix, this is the recipe for you. With tomato, courgette, spinach and beans, it almost takes you over the line for your 5-veg-a-day target.

1. Place beans and their canning liquid, tomatoes and their juices, courgettes and paprika in a large saucepan.

2. Bring to a simmer and cook uncovered for about 10 minutes or until courgette is soft.

3. Add spinach and continue to cook, stirring, until the spinach is just wilted – about a minute or so.

4. Taste, season and serve drizzled generously with your best peppery extra virgin olive oil.

## variations:

**No smoked paprika?** Replace with regular paprika or try ground cumin or coriander.

**Moroccan:** turn it into a vegetable tajine by replacing the paprika with ¼ of a preserved lemon, finely sliced, and using chickpeas instead of the beans.

**Different veg:** pretty much any vegetables you like can be added, including carrots, broccoli and red or green peppers.

**Hot!** Add some fresh or dried chilli or serve with a generous drizzle of chilli oil.

10-minute trick:

Slice the courgettes finely
so they cook more quickly.

# creamed spinach
## with chickpeas

**serves 2**

- 2 cloves garlic, finely sliced
- 250g frozen spinach, thawed
- 400g can chickpeas, drained
- 4–6 tablespoons whipping cream
- lemon juice

OK, I know creamed spinach sounds a little dated, like something out of a bad 70s dinner party menu, but bear with me. This dish was inspired by the creamed spinach at Rockpool Bar & Grill in Melbourne. I love when a simple side dish blows you away.

And while world-famous chefs tend to care about your taste buds and not your waistline, I'm in the business of pleasing both. So I've toned back the cream and added some chickpeas to make for a more substantial meal. Enjoy.

1. Heat a few tablespoons olive oil in a large frying pan.

2. Cook garlic on a medium-high heat for about 30 seconds or until browned.

3. Add spinach and stir-fry for a few minutes until the water has evaporated and the spinach is hot.

4. Stir in chickpeas and cream and cook until hot.

5. Stir in a squeeze of lemon. Taste and season.

variations:

**Dairy-free/vegan:** try coconut milk instead of the cream and consider skipping the lemon juice.

**Fresh spinach:** replace the frozen with a large bunch of fresh spinach or chard. Make sure the leaves are well washed and sliced.

**Side dish:** skip the chickpeas and use as a warming side anywhere you'd think about serving a green salad.

**Short on time?** Skip the garlic.

# asparagus with ricotta and mint

- 2 bunches asparagus, woody bottoms snapped off
- zest of 1 lemon
- 200g ricotta
- 4 sprigs mint, leaves picked

Asparagus was my Mum's favourite vegetable and I seem to have inherited her predilection for it. One day I plan to have a vegetable patch with a generous plot of asparagus.

This is one of my favourite ways to eat it, a simple dish where it is well and truly the star of the show.

1. Bring a large saucepan with about 5cm of salted water in it to the boil.

2. Simmer asparagus for about 5 minutes, until cooked but still with some bite.

3. Drain asparagus and toss with half the zest and 2 tablespoons of extra virgin olive oil. Season.

4. Divide ricotta between 2 plates. Top with mint leaves, the asparagus and the rest of the lemon zest and drizzle with a little extra virgin olive oil.

variations:

**Dairy-free/vegan:** replace the ricotta with a good-quality commercial hummus.

**Different herbs:** basil or flat-leaf parsley will be just as good.

**No asparagus?** I tend to eat this only in the springtime when asparagus is at its best. At other times, green beans or mange tout work well – just adjust the cooking time to suit.

**Higher protein:** a fried or poached egg can be a lovely accompaniment.

# brussels sprouts
## *with* prosciutto

serves 2

- 300g brussels sprouts, trimmed and thinly sliced
- 2 cloves garlic, finely sliced
- 400g can butter beans, drained
- 1–2 tablespoons sherry vinegar
- handful finely sliced prosciutto

I've managed to convert quite a few brussels sprouts haters with this method of cooking them, so if you're unsure – give it a go! Just discard the darker coloured leaves when trimming the brussels as they have the strongest flavour.

The butter beans are here to make more of a complete meal, but if you're cooking for a bean-hater, feel free to skip them.

1. Heat a few tablespoons olive oil in a large frying pan over a medium-high heat.

2. Add brussels sprouts and garlic and stir-fry until sprouts are browned on the edges and almost cooked through – about 3–4 minutes.

3. Toss in beans and continue to stir-fry until they are hot.

4. Remove from the heat. Taste and season with salt, pepper and sherry vinegar.

5. Layer over prosciutto slices and serve hot.

## variations:

**Vegetarian:** replace the prosciutto with some shaved parmesan or even a sharp blue cheese, or serve with a poached egg on top.

**Vegan:** replace prosciutto with a generous handful of roasted almonds or pecans.

**Butter-bean-free?** Use about 200g short pasta or gnocchi that has been cooked according to the packet directions.

**Budget:** prosciutto can be expensive, so feel free to brown some bacon in the pan as a more cost-effective option.

# winter veg stir-fry

serves 2

- 1–2 carrots, peeled and cut into thin batons
- ¼ of a white or Chinese cabbage, sliced into ribbons
- 300g firm tofu, sliced
- 1 teaspoon Chinese five-spice
- 2–3 tablespoons soy sauce

The real driving force behind the wintry vibe of this dish is the Chinese five-spice. It's a blend of, you guessed it, five spices: cinnamon, star anise, cloves, fennel and black pepper. If you can't find it, you could make your own by combining equal parts of the above, or just use twice as much black pepper as cinnamon to make a simpler version.

1. Heat a wok on a fierce heat.

2. Add a little oil and stir-fry the carrots until browned.

3. Add the cabbage and stir-fry for a few minutes or until just starting to soften.

4. Add the tofu and stir-fry for another few minutes or until tofu is hot.

5. Stir in five-spice and season with a generous splash of soy.

## variations:

**Carnivore:** replace the tofu with finely sliced chicken thighs or steak. Stir-fry the meat first until just cooked and then remove to a clean bowl. Continue as per the recipe and add the meat at step 4.

**Herby:** serve sprinkled with flat-leaf parsley or mint.

**Hot!** Add a few finely sliced red chillies with the tofu.

**Different veg:** brussels sprouts are lovely cooked like this, but also consider parsnips, turnip or swede. Tougher root veg may need to be simmered before stir-frying.

**Soy-free:** replace the soy sauce with fish sauce or oyster sauce, and replace the tofu with chicken, beef or pork, or a very large handful of roasted cashews or almonds.

# pasta *and* noodles

# pasta with crushed peas and ricotta

serves 2

- 150g short pasta
- 200g frozen peas
- small bunch mint, leaves picked
- 100g ricotta
- 2 handfuls grated parmesan

I love ricotta. It's such a versatile cheese. From dessert to snacks to main courses, there are few things that don't benefit from a little added creamy cheesiness. But all ricottas are not created equal. I'm always disappointed with the wateriness of ricotta sold in individual tubs in the supermarket. For me it's always worth the hassle to queue at the deli counter to get a slab of real ricotta.

The method for this is a bit fiddly because I wanted to crush the peas, but if you'd prefer to keep it simple, just pop the peas in with the pasta and skip the crushing step.

1. Bring a medium saucepan of salted water to the boil. Add pasta and set timer for the cooking time stated on the packet.

2. When there are 3 minutes to go, add peas, keeping them separate in a sieve.

3. When the timer is up, reserve some cooking water in a cup, then drain peas and pasta, keeping them separate.

4. Return the pan to the heat and add 2 tablespoons olive oil. Add peas and mint. Crush with the back of a fork.

5. Stir in ricotta and drained pasta, adding a little of the cooking water if it seems too dry. Taste, season and serve with parmesan.

variations:

**Vegan/dairy-free:** replace ricotta with a generous drizzle of extra virgin olive oil.

**Carnivore:** pan-fry a couple of crumbled pork sausages and toss in at the end.

**Gluten-free:** chop up ½ a head cauliflower into florets and use in place of the pasta, or replace pasta with a drained can of cannellini or butter beans.

**Super cheesy:** serve with extra freshly grated parmesan.

10-minute trick:

Choose a faster-cooking pasta shape to keep it speedy.
And get things going with boiling water from the kettle.

10-minute trick:

The focus here is on getting the chicken cooked, so make sure it is in the pan before the noodles hit the water.

# chicken *and* lime 2 minute noodles

serves 2

- 300g minced chicken
- 150g 2 minute (ramen) noodles
- 4 tablespoons lime juice + lime halves, to serve
- 4 tablespoons fish sauce
- 1 bunch coriander, leaves picked

When I was at uni, 2 minute (or ramen) noodles were a big staple. I hadn't eaten them for years but decided to give them a go for a piece I was writing about simple noodle dishes. I was amazed how delicious they were when dressed up with a few Thai-inspired ingredients. This version is lovely and fresh, with lime and coriander.

1. Bring a medium saucepan of salted water to the boil.

2. Heat a few tablespoons peanut or other vegetable oil in a large frying pan.

3. Stir-fry chicken for a few minutes over a medium-high heat until browned and cooked through.

4. Boil noodles for 2 minutes. Drain.

5. Toss noodles in with the chicken along with the lime juice and fish sauce. Cook for a minute or so.

6. Taste, season and serve with the coriander.

variations:

**Gluten-free:** replace noodles with rice noodles or mung bean (cellophane) noodles cooked according to the packet directions. Or use a drained can of butter beans instead.

**Vegan:** replace chicken with crumbled tofu.

**Vegetarian:** scramble 3–4 eggs in the usual way then toss in the hot noodles and other ingredients.

**Hot!** Toss in a few super finely sliced fresh red chillies.

# the 'pork fest' pasta with chorizo and bacon

- 3 rashers bacon, chopped
- 1 small chorizo, finely sliced into coins
- 1 clove garlic, finely sliced
- 200g fresh pasta
- 2 tablespoons chopped chives

My Irishman and I recently went vegetarian for a whole month, and while it was a fun and interesting experience, it confirmed our desire to be omnivores. The thing we most missed was pork in all its forms. Our first breakfast back on the meat was a decadent bacon sandwich.

This pasta is a celebration of the goodness of the humble pig. Feel free to play around with the combination of pork products. Some jamón or prosciutto would be a lovely textural contrast, or even some chunky, rustic pork sausage. So much pork, so little time.

1. Bring a medium saucepan of salted water to the boil.

2. Heat a few tablespoons olive oil in a large frying pan or skillet.

3. Fry bacon, chorizo and garlic until well browned.

4. Cook pasta for 2 minutes. Reserve some of the cooking water, then drain.

5. Toss pasta into the frying pan. Stir and add a little reserved cooking water if it looks too dry.

6. Taste and season. Sprinkle with chives.

## variations:

**Vegan:** try a 'tomato-fest' pasta instead. Replace the bacon with a punnet of halved cherry tomatoes and replace the chorizo with a handful of semi- or sun-dried tomatoes.

**Vegetarian:** I'd highly recommend a 'cheese-fest' pasta. Toss the cooked pasta with the sautéed garlic, then remove from the heat and stir in a handful of ricotta and another of finely grated cheddar or parmesan.

**Gluten-free:** use gluten-free pasta or replace with cooked rice noodles or a drained can of butter beans or chickpeas.

**A little healthier:** toss in a few handfuls of baby spinach instead of or as well as the chives.

10-minute trick:

Fresh pasta cooks in a fraction of the time of dried, but it's still best to get the pasta water on to boil before you make the sauce.

# linguine *with* instant 'pesto'

- 200g linguine, or other pasta
- small bunch basil, leaves picked and torn
- 1 small clove garlic, finely chopped
- small handful pinenuts
- 2 handfuls grated parmesan

The idea behind this simple pasta was to deconstruct pesto. Rather than taking the time to pre-blend the basil, garlic, pinenuts and parmesan, I've just added them all to hot pasta. The result is a fresher, lighter, more fragrant dish. Too easy.

1. Bring a medium saucepan of salted water to the boil.

2. Cook pasta according to the packet directions.

3. Scoop out a cupful of cooking water. Drain the pasta.

4. Return pasta to the hot pot with the basil, garlic, pinenuts, parmesan and 2 tablespoons extra virgin olive oil.

5. Stir until the basil is wilted. If it looks too dry, add some of the reserved cooking water or a little more oil.

6. Taste and season.

variations:

**Gluten-free:** use gluten-free pasta or rice noodles. Or my favourite option, a drained can of butter beans.

**Carnivore:** toss in some cooked chicken or finely sliced prosciutto.

**Vegan/dairy-free:** ditch the parmesan, increase the amount of pinenuts and add a squeeze of lemon.

**Double pesto:** serve with a generous dollop of regular pesto on top.

# hokkien noodles with minced beef

- 200g fresh hokkien or Singapore noodles
- 250g minced beef
- 6 spring onions, finely sliced
- 1 bunch baby bok choy, leaves separated
- 4 tablespoons sweet soy sauce or oyster sauce

This is an Asian-inspired version of the great pseudo-Italian dish spaghetti bolognese. It's got all the comforting elements: the soft egg noodles and the minced beef. There's a slight sweetness to the sauce and the wilted bok choy adds some vegetable crunch.

The beauty of this dish is its simplicity. No need to cry while you're chopping the onions. No need to simmer for hours to reduce the sauce. But don't think it doesn't pack a punch in the flavour department. It's seriously good.

1. Place noodles in a heatproof bowl and cover with boiling water. Allow to stand.

2. Heat 2 tablespoons olive oil in a large frying pan or wok. Stir-fry beef over a high heat, until well browned.

3. Add spring onion and bok choy and stir-fry until just wilted.

4. Turn down the heat and add sauce and drained noodles. Cook until everything is hot. Taste and season.

## variations:

**Gluten-free:** replace the hokkien noodles with cooked rice noodles or a drained can of cannellini beans.

**Vegan/vegetarian:** replace beef with crumbled firm tofu, increase the sauce and make sure your 'oyster' sauce is vegetarian – it does exist!

**Can't find fresh noodles?** Use dried noodles or spaghetti cooked according to the packet directions.

**Different veg:** use fresh broccoli instead of, or as well as, the bok choy. Chinese broccoli or purple-sprouting would also work.

**10-minute trick:**

You want to get the beef in the pan before you start prepping the bok choy and spring onions so it has time to get well browned.

10-minute trick:

Chop the cavolo nero finely
to minimise cooking time.

# tagliatelle with greens and almonds

serves 2

- 2 cloves garlic, finely sliced
- 1 large bunch cavolo nero or similar, chopped into thick ribbons
- 200g fresh pasta
- 2 handfuls whole almonds
- squeeze of lemon

Fresh pasta can be a big life saver when you're in a hurry as it only takes a couple of minutes to cook. Of course you could substitute dried pasta if you prefer.

I love to make this dish when I'm feeling like I want the comfort of pasta combined with the healthiness of a veggie dish that focuses on greens.

1. Bring a medium saucepan of salted water to the boil.

2. Meanwhile, heat a few tablespoons olive oil in a large frying pan.

3. Cook garlic for about 30 seconds or until starting to brown.

4. Add greens and allow to wilt. Remove from the heat.

5. Cook pasta for 2 minutes or according to the packet directions. Drain.

6. Toss pasta through cavolo nero and add almonds. Season with salt, pepper and a drizzle of lemon.

variations:

**Vegan:** just use dried pasta (that doesn't contain egg) and adjust cooking times accordingly.

**Different veg:** feel free to use whatever greens you like. Spinach would be lovely or even some curly kale or chard.

**Nut-free:** replace almonds with 2 small handfuls of breadcrumbs that have been toasted at step 3 with the garlic, removed and kept on paper towel while you continue to cook the spinach, and then added at step 5.

**Gluten-free:** use rice noodles or a drained can of chickpeas instead of the pasta.

# noodles *with* tuna *and* tomato

serves 2

- 185g can tuna in oil
- 250g cherry tomatoes, halved
- ¼ of a red onion, finely chopped
- 150g 2-minute (ramen) noodles
- 4 sprigs flat-leaf parsley, leaves picked

When I was little, I used to have this thing where I thought tinned tuna and tomato weren't meant to be together in the same dish. Then I travelled to Italy and accidentally ordered a pasta dish with said ingredients. It blew me away how right they were together. The Italians taught me that the secret to marrying tuna and tomato is to use fresh tomatoes. Simple.

I'm going through a bit of a retro 2-minute (ramen) noodle phase at the moment. By all means use some more respectable pasta if you like.

1. Bring a medium saucepan of salted water to the boil.

2. Heat a large frying pan on medium-high heat.

3. Add the contents of the tuna can, tomatoes and onion.

4. Cook for 5 minutes or until tomatoes have started to break down into a sauce.

5. Meanwhile boil noodles for 2 minutes. Drain.

6. Toss noodles into the sauce.

7. Taste, season and serve with parsley.

variations:

**Vegan:** replace tuna with crumbled tofu or seitan.

**Vegetarian:** skip the tuna and serve with goat's cheese or feta crumbled over the top with the parsley.

**Fresh pasta:** replace the noodles with some fresh fettuccini or tagliatelle. Cook according to the packet directions.

**Gluten-free:** replace noodles with cooked quinoa or brown rice.

# fresh pasta with bocconcini, basil and red peppers

serves 2

- 200g fresh pasta
- 150g jar roasted red peppers, drained and cut into ribbons
- handful bocconcini, torn
- handful fresh basil leaves, torn
- lemon juice

While I love making fresh pasta from scratch and playing around with my pasta machine like an old Italian *nonna,* I don't always have the time. Luckily, commercial fresh pastas tend to be pretty good.

The biggest bonus of using fresh pasta is the wonderful silky texture that tends to be more satisfying than dried pasta. The second biggest bonus is that it only takes a couple of minutes to cook. Perfect for when you're in a hurry.

1. Bring a medium saucepan of salted water to the boil.

2. Cook pasta for 2 minutes or until cooked to your liking. Drain into a colander.

3. Return saucepan to the heat and add 2 tablespoons extra virgin olive oil. Cook peppers for a minute to warm them up.

4. Add drained pasta, bocconcini and basil. Stir.

5. Remove from the heat. Taste and season with salt, pepper and a little lemon juice.

variations:

**Vegan/dairy-free:** replace the bocconcini with a punnet of halved fresh cherry tomatoes or a handful of sun-dried or semi-dried tomatoes.

**Different herbs:** try flat-leaf parsley or finely chopped chives instead of the basil.

**Gluten-free:** chop up ½ a head cauliflower into florets and use in place of the pasta, or replace pasta with a drained can of cannellini or butter beans.

**Luxe:** replace bocconcini with super-fresh Italian buffalo mozzarella.

# buttered courgettes
## with soba noodles

- 4 tablespoons butter
- 4 courgettes, sliced into thin coins
- 2 small cloves garlic, finely sliced
- 150g soba noodles
- 2 large handfuls grated parmesan

Now I don't like to play favourites with my food, especially not my noodles, but soba are up there as one of the best. While they are traditionally a Japanese noodle, I like to mix it up and use them with more Mediterranean-type sauces, like these lovely buttery, melting courgettes, given a kick with some garlic and a little parmesan. So good.

Of course if you can't find soba noodles, this dish would also be lovely with regular old spaghetti. For a vegan version, replace the butter and cheese with a generous pour of fruity olive oil.

1. Bring a medium saucepan of salted water to the boil.

2. Heat a large frying pan on a medium-high heat.

3. Melt butter and stir-fry courgettes and garlic for about 6 minutes or until courgettes are tender.

4. Meanwhile, simmer soba for 4 minutes or until al dente. Drain.

5. Toss hot noodles through the courgettes with the parmesan. Taste and season.

variations:

Vegan/dairy-free: skip the parmesan and replace the butter with a top quality extra virgin olive oil.

Can't find soba noodles? Use hokkien or udon noodles or even dried spaghetti, and cook according to the packet directions.

Gluten-free: use gluten-free pasta or a drained can of lentils.

Super cheesy: serve with fresh ricotta as well as the grated parmesan.

10-minute trick:

The courgettes are the bottle-neck here, so make sure you slice them finely.

# pappardelle *with* smoked salmon *and* ricotta

serves 2

- 150g pappardelle or other pasta
- 60g smoked salmon, torn into chunks
- 200g ricotta
- 2 tablespoons lemon juice + zest of 1 lemon
- 2 tablespoons finely chopped chives

For me there's always something that feels a little fancy when smoked salmon is around. But it keeps for ages in the fridge and can be found in most supermarkets, so it can be a great way to get a bit more fish in your diet if you don't live near a good fishmonger.

If you can't find fat ribbons of pappardelle, tagliatelle or some short pastas like penne or rigatoni would also be perfect.

1. Bring a medium saucepan of salted water to the boil.

2. Cook pasta according to the packet directions or until al dente.

3. Scoop out a cup of the cooking water then drain the pasta.

4. Return pasta to the hot pan then stir in the salmon, ricotta, lemon zest and juice and 2 tablespoons extra virgin olive oil.

5. If it looks a little dry, add some of the reserved cooking water.

6. Taste, season and serve sprinkled with chives.

variations:

**Vegan:** replace the salmon with chopped grilled red peppers and replace the ricotta with a generous drizzle of extra virgin olive oil.

**Vegetarian:** replace the salmon with a handful of semi-dried tomatoes.

**Gluten-free:** chop up ½ a head of cauliflower into florets and use in place of the pasta, or use a drained can of cannellini or butter beans.

**No chives?** Just skip them or replace with flat-leaf parsley.

10-minute trick:

Fresh pasta will cook much
faster than dried.

# grains and legumes

# red lentils with tomato and spinach

## serves 2

- 2 cloves garlic, finely sliced
- 150g red lentils
- 3 tablespoons tomato paste
- handful whole almonds, optional
- 2 large handfuls baby spinach leaves

I wasn't a big fan of red lentils because I found they often ended up mushy. Then I discovered the secret was to only cook them for a short while so they kept their shape. Win-win, really.

This is a great thing to make when you've been over-indulging and are in need of something hearty and healthy – or if you're in the mood to dabble in a little veganism.

The almonds add a lovely crunch but, if you're serving people with allergies, it's equally delicious without.

1. Heat 2 tablespoons olive oil in a large frying pan.

2. Cook garlic over a high heat for about 30 seconds, or until starting to brown.

3. Add lentils, tomato paste and 375ml water. Simmer for about 8 minutes, covered, or until lentils are just cooked, but still al dente.

4. Add almonds and spinach. Stir until the spinach is just wilted.

5. Taste and season.

## variations:

**Nut-free:** skip the almonds or replace with finely diced red pepper for crunch.

**Different lentils:** try puy, green or brown lentils and adjust the cooking time accordingly – around 20 minutes.

**Frozen spinach:** feel free to replace the baby spinach with a block of frozen spinach. Just add it with the tomatoes and simmer a little longer to allow it to defrost.

**Herby:** serve with basil or parsley leaves sprinkled over.

*10-minute trick:*

Lentils are the slow-pokes here, so boil the kettle and make sure you simmer with the lid on to speed things up.

# butter bean 'carbonara'

- 4 rashers bacon, chopped
- 4 egg yolks
- 8 brazil nuts, finely grated
- 2 x 400g cans butter beans, drained
- baby spinach, to serve

This dish was inspired by the classic pasta dish with its sauce of egg yolk, parmesan and bacon. To make a low-GI version we're replacing the pasta with butter beans and the parmesan with shaved brazil nuts.

In fact, feel free to use butter beans or other beans in place of pasta for a healthier take on any of your favourite pasta recipes.

1. Heat a medium frying pan on a high heat.

2. Add a few tablespoons olive oil to the pan. Add bacon and cook for a few minutes until crisp.

3. Meanwhile, combine yolks and grated brazil buts in a medium bowl. Season.

4. When the bacon is crisp, add beans to the pan and stir-fry until hot.

5. Toss the hot beans and bacon into the egg mixture. Serve with spinach on the side.

## variations:

**Vegan:** replace the egg yolk and bacon with chunks of avocado. Either serve cold or pan-fry the beans until hot and then toss into the avocado, brazil nuts and baby spinach.

**Vegetarian:** replace the bacon with a handful of semi-dried tomatoes and the brazil nuts with freshly grated parmesan.

**Healthier:** toss in a handful of raw cauliflower florets with the butter beans.

**Nut-free:** use freshly grated parmesan instead of the brazil nuts.

# red kidney beans with tuna and cherry tomatoes

**serves 2**

- 185g can tuna in oil
- 250g cherry tomatoes, halved
- 2 teaspoons smoked paprika
- 400g can red kidney beans, drained
- 2 sprigs flat-leaf parsley, chopped

For some reason I've harboured a bit of a phobia about red kidney beans. I think it has something to do with the word 'kidney', which instantly reminds me of the overpowering lamb kidneys my mum used to cook for my dad.

Thankfully I've since realised that these little, intensely coloured beans are delicious and bear no resemblance to offal in any form. That being said, I've often made this dish happily with canned butter beans.

1. Heat a frying pan or skillet on a medium-high heat.

2. Add the whole contents of the tuna can, tomatoes and paprika.

3. Cook, stirring occasionally for about 5 minutes or until the tomatoes are starting to break down into a sauce.

4. Add beans and cook until warm.

5. Taste, season and toss in parsley.

variations:

**Vegan:** replace the tuna with crumbled tofu or grilled aubergine from the deli.

**Vegetarian:** skip the tuna and serve with bocconcini torn over at the end.

**Can't find smoked paprika?** Use regular paprika or replace with a smoked or regular mild chilli powder.

**Different herbs?** Try fresh basil or mint instead of the parsley.

# lentils *with* spinach

- 250g fresh or frozen spinach
- 400g can lentils, drained
- 1 tablespoon soy sauce
- 1 tablespoon sherry or other wine vinegar

If canned lentils aren't your thing, feel free to boil some dried brown or green lentils from scratch and use them instead. They usually only take about 20 minutes; just boil and drain when they are tender.

Feel free to play around with the greens. I've used frozen spinach, but fresh spinach would be lovely and will take even less time to cook. Kale, cavolo nero, collard greens and chard are all good too.

1. Put spinach in a medium saucepan with a splash of water. Cover and cook on a medium-high heat for a few minutes.

2. Stir spinach, adding a little more water if the bottom is dry or it's starting to burn.

3. Cover and cook for a few more minutes.

4. When the spinach is warm and any chunks of frozen spinach are gone, add the lentils and cook until warm.

5. Remove from the heat and season with soy, vinegar and 2 tablespoons extra virgin olive oil.

## variations:

**Carnivore:** lovely with a little prosciutto or jamón draped over the top, or with some crumbled and pan-fried pork sausages.

**Spice it up:** when you're feeling adventurous, try adding a teaspoon of ground cumin or coriander when you add the lentils.

**More substantial:** it's pretty substantial already, but you could also stir in a handful of brazil nuts or almonds at the end.

**Soy-free:** either replace the soy sauce with a splash of fish sauce or just skip it and season more generously with sea salt.

# *the* minimalist lentil burger

serves 2

- 3 English muffins
- 400g can lentils, drained
- 1 teaspoon baharat, ground cumin or coriander
- mayonnaise, to serve
- mixed salad leaves, to serve

Now don't get me wrong, I love a good beef burger as much as the next girl, but the first time I made these lentil burgers I was amazed not only at how good they were, but also at how much they looked like a normal burger. I'd even venture so far as to say that they would satisfy even the most hardened carnivore – although I should try them on my brother and report back.

Baharat is a wonderful Lebanese spice blend that contains black pepper, cumin, coriander, cinnamon, paprika and cardamom. If you don't have any handy, ground cumin or coriander would be a good substitute.

I like English muffins for my burgers because they're not too big and are easy to get hold of, but please feel free to use your favourite burger bun or a panini.

1. In a food processor whizz one of the muffins until you have chunky breadcrumbs.

2. Add half the lentils, the spice and a little salt. Whizz until you have a smooth-ish paste.

3. Add remaining lentils. Pulse until combined, but still chunky. Taste, season and form into two burger patties.

4. Heat oil to cover the base of a frying pan and cook burgers about 2 minutes each side, or until brown.

5. Generously slather the insides of the remaining muffins with mayo.

6. Add the burgers and leaves. Sandwich together.

## variations:

**Vegan:** serve with vegan mayonnaise or hummus.

**Carnivore:** replace the lentils with minced beef, although you may need to cook the burgers for longer.

**Gluten-free:** replace the English muffin used for the patty with 90g cooked brown rice, then simply serve the burgers on a bed of salad leaves with the mayo generously dolloped on top.

10-minute trick:

Use a higher heat for the aubergine and stir more frequently to make it cook even quicker. And remember to use a lid.

# chickpea *and* aubergine tortillas

serves 2

- 1 aubergine, diced
- 400g can chickpeas, drained
- 6 tortillas or pita bread
- small bunch mint, leaves picked
- mayonnaise or natural yoghurt, to serve

The challenge with this recipe is to get the aubergine cooked in 10 minutes. It can be done, but there's nothing worse than undercooked aubergine so make sure it's lovely and silky.

For simplicity I've heated the tortillas in the oven, but you could use the microwave. If you have time, the best method is to heat them individually on a hot pan so you get a few toasty bits.

1. Preheat oven to 200°C.

2. Heat a few tablespoons olive oil in a large frying pan with a lid over medium-high heat.

3. Add aubergine and cook, covered but stirring often, for about 9 minutes or until the aubergine is soft.

4. Add chickpeas and allow to heat for another minute or so. Season well.

5. Meanwhile, wrap tortillas in foil and heat in the oven for a few minutes. Keep warm.

6. Serve the aubergine and chickpeas in a bowl with mint leaves and yoghurt or mayonnaise on the side.

variations:

Vegan: use a vegan mayonnaise or make a sauce from equal parts tahini, lemon juice and water.

Short on time? Replace the fresh aubergine with grilled aubergine from the deli.

Gluten-free: serve with iceberg lettuce leaves to wrap instead of the tortillas.

Hot! Add a little fresh or dried chilli with the chickpeas.

# quinoa with pesto and cauliflower

serves 2

- 90g quinoa
- ½ a large cauliflower (approx. 350g), cut into tiny trees
- 6 tablespoons pesto
- lemon juice
- parmesan shavings, to serve

This recipe is a bit of a struggle to get done in 10 minutes, but it can be done, although if you prefer your quinoa a little softer, just simmer for a few more minutes.

If you haven't cooked with quinoa, I highly recommend tracking some down in the health-food section of your local supermarket, and check out '12 things you should know about quinoa' on Stonesoup.

1. Bring a medium saucepan of salted water to the boil.

2. Cook quinoa for 9 minutes or until tender.

3. Meanwhile, heat a few tablespoons olive oil in a large frying pan over a medium-high heat.

4. Cook cauliflower, covered, stirring every minute or so until brown on the edges and tender. Season.

5. Drain quinoa and toss in the pan with cauliflower, pesto and a squeeze of lemon.

6. Taste and season. Top with parmesan.

variations:

**Different veg:** replace the cauli with broccoli.

**Vegan/dairy-free:** replace the parmesan with a handful of brazil nuts, pinenuts or almonds, and use basil oil instead of the pesto.

**No pesto?** Just stir in a bunch of chopped basil and 3–4 tablespoons of olive oil and increase the parmesan.

**No quinoa?** Replace with another grain like brown rice and adjust the cooking time, or replace with 95g couscous soaked in 125ml boiling water and skip the boiling step.

**10-minute trick:**

Use boiled water from the kettle and be
sure to get the quinoa cooking asap.

# warm salad of lentils and peas

- 250g frozen peas
- 400g can lentils, drained
- 1 tablespoon sherry vinegar
- 1 bunch mint, leaves picked
- 6 slices prosciutto or pancetta

Canned lentils are a relatively recent addition to my cooking repertoire, but the more I use them the more I love them. The trick is not to overcook them as they can turn into a mush. Best to just gently heat them so they keep their shape.

1. Heat a large saucepan on a medium heat.

2. Add a few tablespoons olive oil to the pan and add the peas.

3. Cover and cook for 6–7 minutes until the peas are hot and starting to shrivel a little.

4. Add lentils and cook until hot.

5. Remove from the heat and add vinegar, mint and prosciutto. Taste and season.

## variations:

**Vegetarian:** replace prosciutto with a few hard-boiled eggs sliced in half.

**Vegan:** replace prosciutto with a generous handful of roasted almonds or other nuts.

**Lentil-free:** the salad is lovely without lentils – just increase the peas a little to compensate, and it probably won't need the vinegar.

**Leafy:** toss in a handful of washed and dried salad leaves or baby spinach.

# chicken *and* egg fried rice

- 1 chicken breast, finely sliced into ribbons
- 360g cooked rice, preferably basmati
- 2 eggs, lightly beaten
- 2 tablespoons soy sauce
- 3 spring onions, finely sliced

The name of this dish sounds a bit philosophical. I mean, which came first? But you don't need to be a scholarly type to enjoy the simple, comforting pleasure of fried rice.

On different occasions, I've used par-cooked commercial rice and homemade rice that I've frozen, both with great results. If you do need to cook your rice from scratch, make sure you allow it to cool properly for half an hour before you fry it so that it has time to be in a frying frame of mind.

1. Heat a few tablespoons peanut or other vegetable oil in a large frying pan or wok.

2. Stir-fry chicken over a high heat for a few minutes or until cooked through.

3. Add rice and eggs. Continue to stir-fry until the eggs are set and the rice is hot.

4. Season with soy and serve scattered with the spring onions.

## variations:

**Vegan:** replace eggs and chicken with about 150g smoked tofu, crumbled, and a pinch of chilli flakes and/or ground turmeric.

**Vegetarian:** skip the chicken and increase the eggs to 3 or 4.

**Healthier:** stir-fry a few handfuls of chopped vegetables such as red peppers, carrots, celery, courgettes or peas in with the chicken.

**Rice-free:** replace rice with a drained can of lentils.

**Gluten-free:** replace soy sauce with tamari, a gluten-free soy.

10-minute trick:

The chicken must be cut into thin strips so it cooks quickly.

# warm chickpea salad

serves 1

- 1 clove garlic, finely sliced
- 1 sprig rosemary, leaves picked
- pinch dried chilli flakes, optional
- small handful whole almonds
- 210g can chickpeas, drained

This is a great pantry recipe to have up your sleeve for cooking emergencies.

If you are in the mood for some greenery, a nice little side salad wouldn't go astray, but it is completely satisfying on its own.

1. Heat a medium frying pan over a medium-high heat. Add a few tablespoons olive oil.

2. When the oil is hot add the garlic, rosemary, chilli and almonds (if using) and stir-fry for a minute or so, until the garlic is just starting to brown.

3. Toss through drained chickpeas and continue to stir-fry until chickpeas are warm and starting to brown up a little as well.

4. Season generously and serve warm or at room temperature.

variations:

No rosemary? Fresh thyme or sage are both excellent substitutes.

Nut-free: skip the almonds and serve with finely grated parmesan on the side.

Different legumes: try cannellini, borlotti or butter beans instead of the chickpeas.

Leafy: toss in a handful of salad leaves or flat-leaf parsley.

# veggie chilli

- 2 x 400g cans tomatoes
- 400g can lentils, drained
- 400g can red kidney beans, drained
- 1–2 teaspoons chilli powder
- 3 tablespoons fried onions or shallots (see introduction)

It's hard to beat the winning combo of chilli, beans and tomato. And while chilli con carne can be lovely, I prefer this veggie-friendly version which uses lentils instead of minced beef.

I've recently been using fried onions or shallots from large supermarkets or Asian grocery stores as an instant way to inject some oniony flavour into quick dishes. If you can't find them, just soften an onion in a little oil before processing with the rest of the recipe.

1. Place tomatoes, lentils, beans and chilli in a large saucepan.

2. Simmer over a medium-high heat for about 5 minutes or until the sauce has thickened slightly.

3. Stir in the shallots, leaving a few to sprinkle over the top.

4. Taste and season, adding a little more chilli if it needs it.

variations:

**Carnivore:** brown about 250g minced beef in the pan before adding the other ingredients and skip the lentils or leave them in, as you like.

**No kidney beans?** Replace with white beans, black beans or even chickpeas.

**Smoky:** add a few teaspoons of smoked paprika or use a smoky chilli powder.

**More Mexican:** serve with fresh coriander leaves and a little sour cream.

# home 'baked' chickpeas

**serves 2**

- 400g can chickpeas
- 2 tablespoons tomato paste or ketchup
- 1 teaspoon ground cumin
- 2 generous knobs butter
- 2 handfuls baby spinach

If I was going to play favourites, chickpeas would definitely win a place as my most beloved legume. I think they're underrated as a breakfast food, which is why I came up with this new take on good old baked beans.

This is one of those dishes that is equally at home for breakfast, lunch or dinner.

1. Place chickpeas and the juice from the can in a medium saucepan on a high heat.

2. Add tomato paste, cumin and butter, and simmer for 5 minutes or until the sauce has thickened up a little.

3. Season and serve chickpeas on a bed of baby spinach.

## variations:

Carnivore: brown 1–2 sliced chorizos in the pan before adding the chickpeas and continuing as above.

Vegan/dairy-free: replace the butter with a few generous drizzles of good olive oil.

Hot! Add in a few finely chopped red chillies or some dried chilli powder – ½–1 teaspoon should do it.

Beans: replace chickpeas with canned borlotti beans.

Budget: soak and cook dried chickpeas from scratch, then use about 125ml of their cooking liquid.

# eggs and tofu

# tofu 'ragu' with tomato and peppers

- 150g jar red peppers, drained
- 300g firm tofu, drained and crumbled
- 4 tablespoons tomato paste
- 2 teaspoons smoked paprika
- green leaves, to serve

While I love delicate, silken tofu in my miso soup, firm tofu is my preferred option for cooking with. I find the best firm tofu is the one that feels the firmest in the packet, so go ahead and have a little squeeze in the supermarket.

Feel free to spice this up with a little fresh or dried chilli. With a little extra tomato paste, I'm thinking it would make a wonderful sauce for pasta.

Use this as a vegetarian alternative anywhere you'd use a bolognese sauce.

1. Heat a few tablespoons olive oil in a large frying pan.

2. Add peppers and stir for a few seconds. Add tofu and stir-fry, breaking it up further with a fork or spoon. Cook for a few minutes.

3. Add tomato paste and paprika. Continue to cook and stir for a few more minutes until everything is hot and the tofu is well scrambled.

4. Taste and season. Serve on a bed of greens.

variations:

**Carnivore:** brown about 250g minced beef in the pan before adding the other ingredients. Skip the tofu or leave it in, as you like.

**Can't find smoked paprika?** Just skip it or use regular paprika.

**No peppers?** Use chopped, fresh red peppers instead.

**More substantial:** serve with cooked pasta or on hot buttered toast.

# chilli-spiced tofu
## with hummus

serves 2

- 1 teaspoon dried chilli flakes
- 2 teaspoons smoked paprika
- 4 slices firm tofu (about 300g)
- 6–8 tablespoons hummus
- small bunch coriander, leaves picked

Tofu generally gets a bad rap for being bland, but as I learned when I was vegetarian for a month, it is a wonderful sponge for soaking up flavours.

I love this. The tofu takes on the chilli and smokiness from the paprika and cooks to a lovely reddish-golden crispiness. With the calming influence of hummus and the fresh fragrance of coriander, you have a balanced meal in a bowl.

1. Combine chilli and paprika with 1 tablespoon olive oil. Season and toss tofu slices in the spiced oil to coat.

2. Heat a medium frying pan or skillet on medium-high heat.

3. Cook tofu for a few minutes each side, until crisp on the outside and heated through the middle.

4. Smear hummus over 2 plates. Top with tofu and sprinkle over coriander leaves.

## variations:

Carnivore: replace tofu with steaks and adjust the cooking time so the steaks are cooked to your liking.

No smoked paprika? Just skip it or replace with 1 teaspoon each of ground cumin and coriander.

Different herbs: use mint or flat-leaf parsley instead of the coriander.

More substantial: serve with pita bread.

# crab omelette

serves 2

- 2 tablespoons butter
- 4 eggs
- 170g can crab meat, drained
- small handful flat-leaf parsley, leaves picked

If you haven't ever learned to cook an omelette, I highly recommend giving it a go. Omelettes are one of the most simple, satisfying meals and it's worthwhile having them in your repertoire.

In this version I've used canned crab. It's not exactly a glamorous ingredient, but for me canned crab is better than no crab. If you have access to fresh crab, by all means use it.

1. Heat butter in a small frying pan, skillet or omelette pan over a medium heat.

2. Gently stir eggs for a few seconds, then add to the pan.

3. Cook eggs, stirring, for about 30 seconds, like you're making scrambled eggs.

4. When the egg looks like it's about half set, stop stirring and sprinkle over the drained crab meat.

5. When the egg is mostly cooked through, remove from the heat and season.

6. Turn omelette out onto a plate, folding in half so the crab is in the middle. Sprinkle with parsley.

variations:

**Carnivore:** replace the crab with sliced ham.

**Vegetarian:** skip the crab and use your favourite cheese, or mushrooms, or increase the eggs to 5 or 6.

**More substantial:** serve with a green salad or hot buttered toast, or both!

# crisp tofu *with* white beans and gremolata

serves 2

- small bunch flat-leaf parsley, leaves picked
- zest of 1 lemon
- 1 small clove garlic, sliced finely
- 4 slices tofu (approx. 300g)
- 400g can cannellini or other white beans, drained

With the beans and tofu, this is about as protein-packed as vegetarian (or even vegan) eating gets.

The success of this dish relies on getting the tofu all golden and crispy in the pan, being generous with the salt and pepper, and the flavour explosion of the 'gremolata' – an Italian-inspired combo of parsley, garlic and lemon zest that is often used to freshen up slow-cooked meat dishes.

1. Finely chop the parsley, lemon zest and garlic together.

2. Heat a few tablespoons olive oil in a frying pan over a medium-high heat.

3. Pat tofu slices dry with paper towel. Cook tofu for about 2 minutes on each side or until golden and very crisp. Season well.

4. Divide tofu between 2 warm plates.

5. Add beans to the pan. Stir-fry until warm.

6. Toss about half the parsley mixture in with the beans.

7. Place beans on top of tofu. Sprinkle over remaining parsley mixture.

## variations:

**Carnivore:** replace tofu with chicken breasts or thigh fillets and change the cooking time accordingly.

**Soy-free:** use halloumi instead of the tofu.

**Hot!** Add 1–2 teaspoons chilli powder to the tofu cooking oil.

**Saucy:** serve with a little sour cream.

# spicy mexican breakfast eggs

- 400g can tomatoes, chopped
- 1 teaspoon dried chilli flakes
- 2 tablespoons butter
- 4 eggs
- shaved parmesan, to serve

Huevos rancheros is a classic Mexican breakfast dish where eggs are served with a spicy tomato sauce and often some tortillas.

If you're a little nervous about cooking eggs, this is a great place to start. The tomato helps conduct the heat so the eggs cook more evenly.

I love these eggs served with hot buttered toast and a strong cup of milky tea.

1. Place tomato, chilli and butter in a large frying pan.

2. Bring to a simmer. Cook for about 4 minutes or until starting to reduce into a thicker sauce.

3. Break eggs into the sauce and cook, covered, for another 3–4 minutes or until the whites are set but the yolks are still runny.

4. Season and sprinkle over the cheese.

variations:

**Vegan:** replace eggs with a drained can of white beans and simmer until hot. Skip the cheese.

**Dairy-free:** skip the cheese and use olive oil instead of the butter. Be generous.

**Turkish eggs:** replace the chilli with ground cumin and the parmesan with a soft cheese like goat's cheese or feta.

**More Mexican:** serve with fresh coriander leaves and a little sour cream.

# curried tofu scramble

serves 2

- 1 onion, chopped
- 4 teaspoons curry powder
- 350g firm tofu
- 2 large handfuls baby spinach leaves
- juice of ½ a lemon

This is inspired by Heidi Swanson's recipe in *Super Natural Cooking* and is a great dish for convincing non tofu fans that tofu can be delicious. As Heidi says, she's given up on trying to convince with argument and just slides a plate of this dish in front of her carnivore friends. Few are able to resist the urge to try it!

Don't stress about the type of curry powder. Whatever you have on hand will be wonderful – you may just need to tweak the level to suit your taste.

1. Heat a few tablespoons olive oil in a large frying pan.

2. Add onion and cook, covered, over a medium-high heat, stirring frequently until the onion is soft and translucent but not browned.

3. Add curry powder and stir-fry for about 30 seconds or until it smells divine.

4. Crumble the tofu with your hands and add to the pan. Stir well, then cover and cook for a few minutes – you just want to warm the tofu through.

5. Add spinach and stir until the spinach has just started to wilt.

6. Season generously with sea salt, pepper and a big squeeze of lemon juice.

## variations:

**Soy-free:** replace the tofu with about 5 eggs. Cook, stirring, over a medium-low heat until the eggs are only just set and serve on a bed of baby spinach. Skip the lemon juice.

**No curry powder?** Make your own with 1 teaspoon each of chilli powder, turmeric, ground coriander and ground cumin.

**Not a curry fan?** Replace the curry powder with 1 teaspoon turmeric for colour without the intense flavour.

**Short on time?** Skip the onion and serve sprinkled with chopped chives.

10-minute trick:

Get the onion cooking asap, using a medium-high heat and stirring frequently.

# mel and carlos' 'green' eggs

- 5–6 eggs
- 2 tablespoons butter
- 3 tablespoons pesto
- 2 handfuls baby spinach, washed

Inspired by a wonderful breakfast hosted by my great Melbourne mates Mel and Carlos. I love it when my friends cook for me and inspire a 'Why didn't I think of that?' moment.

1. Heat a small frying pan on a medium-high heat.

2. Break eggs into a small bowl and stir to just break up the yolks. Season.

3. Add butter to the hot pan and allow to melt a little. Add eggs and cook for about 30 seconds, turning down the heat if they are cooking too fast.

4. Scoop all the cooked egg into the middle of the pan and allow the runny egg to run to the sides.

5. Stir in pesto and continue to cook for another minute or until the eggs are no longer runny. Quickly serve eggs on a bed of baby spinach.

## variations:

**Green eggs and ham:** make like the Dr Seuss book and pan-fry some good-quality leg ham to serve under your eggs.

**Vegan/dairy-free:** try 'green' tofu. Crumble some firm tofu and pan-fry until warm and starting to brown in places. Stir in some dairy-free pesto such as a Sicilian nut pesto made with a few handfuls of almonds instead of the parmesan.

**Budget:** make your own pesto or finely chop a small bunch of parsley and use it instead to make your eggs green.

**Decadent:** add a few tablespoons of sour cream to the eggs for a richer, creamier scrambled egg experience.

**Nut-free:** replace pesto with a small bunch finely chopped basil leaves and a little parmesan if you like.

# fish

# salmon *with* courgettes and brown rice

- 2 courgettes, finely diced
- 200g can salmon, drained
- 360g cooked brown rice
- 2 sprigs flat-leaf parsley, finely chopped
- 2–3 tablespoons lemon juice

This dish was inspired by my snow-bunny sister, who is more into skiing than cooking. Her latest culinary creation is canned tuna, brown rice, ricotta, a little cheddar and sometimes some grated courgette, which she zaps in the microwave until the cheese melts. I need to try her version, but this one, with salmon, is very moreish.

1. Heat a few tablespoons olive oil on a medium-high heat.

2. Cook courgettes for about 5 minutes or until starting to soften.

3. Add salmon and rice. Cook, stirring, until everything is hot and the salmon is broken into small chunks.

4. Remove from the heat. Stir in parsley and lemon juice.

5. Taste and season.

## variations:

**Vegan/vegetarian:** replace the salmon with crumbled tofu or whole almonds.

**Different fish:** canned tuna or sardines will work, or try cooking fresh fish and flaking it into the dish.

**Lower GI:** replace the rice with cooked or canned lentils.

**Short on time?** Finely grate the courgettes so they cook super fast or replace with 2 handfuls of baby spinach leaves tossed in at the end.

fish 201

10-minute trick:

The courgettes take the longest
to cook in this dish, so get them
going before you do anything else.

# salt and pepper squid

- 2 large squid tubes
- 1 tablespoon lemon juice
- 1 tablespoon dijon mustard
- 2 tablespoons flour
- 2 large handfuls mixed salad leaves

I used to be a squid snob and only use fresh squid that I painstakingly cleaned myself. Then my beautiful mate Missy Helgs cooked some frozen squid for me. I was amazed at how tender and delicious it was.

These days I'm happy to use the far less messy frozen option. It's a great thing to have on hand in the freezer for a last-minute seafood dinner – one of those things that tastes and feels way more exotic than it actually is.

1. Prepare the squid by 'scoring' or lightly cutting in a diagonal pattern without cutting all the way through.

2. Whisk together lemon juice, mustard and 3 tablespoons extra virgin olive oil. Season.

3. Put flour in a plastic bag and season with a tablespoon freshly ground pepper and some sea salt flakes.

4. Preheat a large frying pan or skillet with a thin layer of peanut or other frying oil.

5. Toss squid in the flour and shake to remove any excess.

6. Shallow fry until golden-brown on both sides.

7. Serve with leaves and the mustard dressing on the side.

## variations:

**Vegan/vegetarian:** try salt and pepper tofu. Replace the squid with firm tofu, finely sliced into bite-sized pieces.

**Carnivore:** use finely sliced chicken breast (about 400g) instead of the squid and skip the scoring step. Make sure it's cooked through before removing from the pan.

**Chilli:** toss in 1–2 teaspoons of dried chilli flakes or powder with the flour.

**Short on time?** Skip the dressing and serve with a good quality whole-egg mayonnaise and lemon wedges instead.

**Gluten-free:** use a corn- or rice-based flour instead.

# raw salmon *with* couscous *and* mint

- 190g couscous
- ¼ of a small red onion, finely diced
- 300g sashimi grade salmon, finely diced
- 4 tablespoons lemon juice + lemon halves, to serve
- 3 sprigs mint, leaves picked and roughly chopped

This is based on kibbeh, a Middle Eastern dish of raw meat mixed with herbs and bulghur or cracked wheat. Lamb is the most commonly used meat, but I've gone for a lighter option with salmon.

I just love the texture of this dish: chewy couscous with silky raw fish and little crunchy bursts of red onions. So summery and refreshing.

If you're after a more substantial meal, serve with some warmed pita bread. Or you could serve as a starter shared between 4.

1. Combine couscous and 2 tablespoons extra virgin olive oil in a heat-proof bowl.

2. Pour over 250ml boiling water. Cover and allow to stand for 5 minutes.

3. Fluff couscous with a fork and stir in onion, salmon, lemon and mint.

4. Taste and season and serve with lemon wedges.

## variations:

**Vegan/vegetarian:** replace the salmon with a drained can of chickpeas and increase the couscous and water by 95g/125ml each.

**Gluten-free:** replace the couscous and water with a drained can of chickpeas that have been roughly chopped.

**Cooked salmon:** if you can't get sashimi-grade fish, pop the salmon in with the couscous and boiling water so it cooks.

**Budget:** replace salmon with canned tuna in oil.

# seared tuna *and* cherry tomatoes

- 2 tuna steaks, approx. 1cm thick
- 250g cherry tomatoes
- 2 tablespoons capers
- 2 large handfuls wild rocket
- 4 tablespoons mayonnaise

The inspiration for this dish was the wonderful southern French salad, Niçoise. The traditional salad is quite hearty, with tuna, boiled potatoes, green beans, capers, anchovies, olives and boiled eggs. Way more than 5 ingredients. This is my minimalist version.

You can serve the tuna as a whole steak or tear the cooked tuna into chunks, mix it with the tomato, capers and rocket and drizzle over some mayonnaise.

While I love tuna still rare in the middle, I don't like it to be ice cold. So I tend to use thinner steaks rather than the impossible-to-cook doorsteps you often see.

1. Heat a large frying pan or skillet on medium-high heat.

2. Rub tuna with oil. Season.

3. Add fish and tomatoes to the hot pan. Sear for about a minute on each side.

4. Serve steaks sprinkled with capers and tomato. Serve rocket and mayonnaise on the side.

## variations:

**Vegan:** use 2 portobello or field mushrooms per person and sear until tender, about 4 minutes each side. Use a vegan mayo.

**Carnivore:** replace tuna with minute beef steaks.

**Vegetarian:** try halloumi sliced 1cm thick and pan-fried until golden on both sides – about 3 minutes a side.

**Egg-free:** use a vegan mayonnaise or serve with hummus or natural yoghurt instead.

# salmon with asparagus and dill mayonnaise

- 300g salmon fillets
- 1 bunch asparagus
- 1 tablespoon lemon juice + lemon halves, to serve
- 2 tablespoons finely chopped dill
- 4 tablespoons whole-egg mayonnaise

Salmon can be very oily, which is great because it's difficult to over-cook and dry it out. But it can feel a little too rich. This method of cutting the fish into thin scallops or 'minute' steaks means more surface area in contact with the pan, so more chance for the oil to cook out and leave you with lovely crispy bits.

Sea trout is very similar to salmon and I often use them interchangeably, depending on which looks best at the fish market.

1. Bring a large saucepan of salted water to the boil.

2. Cut salmon into thin fillets about 5mm thick. Rub with oil and season.

3. Boil asparagus for about 5 minutes or until tender. Drain.

4. Meanwhile, heat a large frying pan on a medium-high heat. Cook salmon for a minute on each side.

5. Combine lemon juice, dill and mayonnaise. Taste and season.

6. Serve fish topped with asparagus and a dollop of the dill mayo, with lemon wedges on the side.

## variations:

**Vegan/vegetarian:** replace the salmon with firm tofu and use a vegan mayonnaise.

**Different veg:** if asparagus isn't in season replace with broccoli, broccolini or green beans and adjust the cooking time as needed.

**Different herbs:** if you're not keen on dill, try thyme or lemon thyme or even parsley.

**Egg-free:** replace mayo with a creamy natural yoghurt, crème fraiche or sour cream.

# prawn *and* avocado salad

- 10–12 large cooked prawns
- 1 ripe avocado
- juice of 1 lime + 1 lime, to serve
- 2 large handfuls mixed salad leaves
- 1 teaspoon dried chilli flakes

Prawns and avocado are one of the classic food marriages, up there with tomato and basil or rosemary and potatoes.

The chilli flakes give it all a nice sharp fiery kick, but if you're not a hot head, feel free to dial the chilli back or omit it all together.

I like to leave the prawn tails on not only because they look pretty, but because they add a lovely crunchy element. Most people don't eat them, but for me they're the best part of the prawn. I urge you to try them at least once.

1. Peel prawns, leaving the little tails on.

2. Halve avocado and cut into wedges, discarding the peel and the stone.

3. Combine 2 tablespoons lime juice with 2 tablespoons extra virgin olive oil and the chilli flakes. Season.

4. Toss leaves in the dressing and layer on 2 plates.

5. Arrange prawns and avocado on the leaves and serve with extra lime halves.

variations:

**Vegetarian:** replace prawns with 3–4 hard-boiled eggs, peeled and halved.

**Vegan:** use a drained can of white beans or chickpeas or a large handful of almonds instead of the prawns.

**Fancy:** use cooked lobster or crab instead of the prawns.

# sardines *with* chickpeas

serves 2

- 2 tablespoons red wine vinegar
- ¼ of a red onion, finely sliced
- 120g can sardines, drained
- 400g can chickpeas, drained
- small bunch flat-leaf parsley, leaves picked

This salad has all my favourite things: chickpeas, sardines, vinegar – yum. It won't be for everyone, but if you're like me and have a passion for sardines, you'll enjoy this as a change from boring old sardines on toast.

Recently, my dad and I did a tasting of all the different sardines from the local supermarket. It was pretty amazing how different the different brands were. If you're super lucky and have access to fresh sardine fillets, by all means cook them under the grill and use them here instead.

1. Mix vinegar with 2 tablespoons extra virgin olive oil. Season.

2. Toss in onion, sardines, chickpeas and parsley and gently combine.

3. Taste and season.

variations:

**Not a sardine fan?** If I can't convince you, use canned tuna in oil instead.

**Vegetarian:** replace sardines with some torn bocconcini or buffalo mozzarella.

**Vegan:** replace the sardines with a large handful of roasted cashews.

**Healthier:** toss in a handful of finely chopped raw broccoli.

# classic mussels
## *with* white wine

- ½ glass dry white wine
- 1–2 cloves garlic
- generous knob butter + extra, to serve
- 1kg mussels
- crusty bread, to serve

I almost didn't include this recipe in the book because it has been done a million times. But I love mussels and it didn't seem right to leave them out of the seafood section.

For the whole Belgian experience, serve with hot potato chips. For the best cooking method for the perfect chip, check out my article on Stonesoup: 'Cold-oil potato chips'.

1. Put wine, garlic and butter in a large saucepan and bring to the boil over the highest heat.

2. Add mussels and jam the lid on.

3. Cook for a couple of minutes, then remove the lid and pull out any mussels that have opened.

4. Return the lid and cook for another few minutes. Remove any more opened mussels. Repeat once more.

5. Discard any unopened mussels and return the opened ones to the pan. Heat for half a minute.

6. Serve hot with bread and butter.

variations:

**Dairy-free:** you guessed it – olive oil instead of the butter!

**Alcohol-free:** use water or verjuice instead of the wine.

**Gluten-free:** serve with commercial potato chips or crisps.

# buttery garlicky grilled prawns

- 10–12 large raw prawns (approx. 500g)
- 2 cloves garlic, finely sliced
- 2 generous knobs of butter, chopped
- lemon, to serve
- crusty bread, to serve

Prawns + butter + garlic = a classic combination. And there's a very good reason for that – they're finger-licking delicious, and some would say addictive.

It's not that often that I cook prawns because they can be such a pain to peel. For me, peeling prawns for others is an act of selfless love. Fortunately this recipe overcomes the prawn-peeling drama by getting everyone to do their own.

The garlic level in this recipe is relatively moderate. Feel free to increase it as much as you dare. A sprinkling of dried chilli flakes wouldn't go astray either.

1. Preheat an overhead grill on its highest setting.

2. Place prawns in a heat-proof dish and scatter with garlic and the butter.

3. Grill for about 4 minutes, turning halfway, until prawns have changed colour and look cooked.

4. Plonk the pan in the middle of the table and serve with lemon quarters, bread, an empty bowl for the prawn shells and lots of serviettes for garlicky fingers.

## variations:

**Vegetarian:** if there's one thing that loves butter and garlic as much as prawns, it's mushrooms, so use about 4 large field mushrooms and cook until tender, around 10 minutes or a little longer.

**Vegan:** as per the vegetarian option but use olive oil instead of the butter.

**Gluten-free:** serve with a huge green salad instead of the bread and butter.

**Barbecue:** feel free to barbecue the prawns then let the butter and garlic melt over them.

# fish steaks with olive tapenade

- 2 fish steaks (see introduction)
- 4 large handfuls baby spinach, or other greens
- lemon juice
- 4 tablespoons olive tapenade

While I adore swordfish, I try to eat it only every now and then because it tends to have high levels of mercury. Tuna or marlin steaks would work here, as would salmon cutlets. Halibut would be a good northern hemisphere choice.

Olive tapenade may seem like a strange accompaniment to fish, but it is delicious with the more robust, meaty fish steaks. Somehow the olive intensity brightens and complements the fish in a similar way to lemon juice.

This is a wonderful winter fish dish. For something even more comforting, serve with hot, buttery mashed potato.

1. Preheat a large frying pan on a high heat.

2. Rub fish generously with olive oil. Season.

3. Cook fish for about 1½ minutes each side, or until cooked to your liking.

4. Remove fish from the pan. Add baby spinach. Stir and cook until wilted. Splash with a little lemon juice.

5. Combine tapenade with 2 tablespoons extra virgin olive oil and 1 tablespoon lemon juice.

6. Serve fish on a bed of wilted greens with the tapenade on top.

variations:

Vegan: use 2 portobello or field mushrooms per person and sear until tender, about 4 minutes each side.

Carnivore: replace fish with minute beef steaks.

Vegetarian: try halloumi, sliced 1cm thick, and pan-fried until golden on both sides – about 3 minutes a side.

Tapenade alternatives: try pesto, hummus or aioli.

# fish tacos

serves 2

- 4 tortillas
- large bunch coriander
- juice + zest of 1 lime
- 300g fish fillets (see introduction)
- aioli, to serve

Flathead is my all-time favourite fish for this recipe; whiting is another winner, but any white fish fillets would be fine. If you don't have access to a good fishmonger, chicken breasts would also work well.

I think these are best served with aioli – garlicky mayonnaise. But if you'd prefer a more virtuous option, natural yoghurt is also delicious.

1. Preheat oven to 200°C. Wrap the tortillas in foil and pop in the oven to warm up.

2. Finely chop coriander stems and half the leaves. Combine with lime zest, juice and 4 tablespoons olive oil.

3. Coat fish in the marinade.

4. Preheat a large frying pan with a thin layer of olive oil on medium-high heat.

5. Cook fish for a few minutes on each side.

6. Serve fish with warm tortillas, aioli and remaining coriander leaves, for everyone to wrap their own.

## variations:

**Vegetarian/vegan:** replace the fish with firm tofu. And for vegans use a vegan mayonnaise mixed with a little fresh garlic instead of the aioli.

**Egg-free:** serve with sour cream or natural yoghurt instead of the mayo.

**Short on time?** Whizz the marinade ingredients in a food processor instead of chopping. The downside is you'll have more washing up.

**Gluten-free:** serve with steamed rice or cooked lentils instead of the tortillas.

# meat and poultry

# chicken with green beans and pesto

serves 2

- 1 large (approx. 250g) chicken breast, cut in half
- 1 teaspoon dried chilli flakes
- 250g green beans, stalks removed, pretty tails left on
- 4 tablespoons pesto
- 1 lemon, halved on the diagonal

I used to hate green beans when I was little, almost as much as I detested peas. The beans of my childhood were always frozen, and I still feel a bit funny about them. But fresh green beans are a whole other story – a thing of beauty.

If you're going to go for store-bought pesto, I highly recommend seeking out one from the chiller section. My Irishman and I did a tasting of commercial pestos recently, and while the jars were pretty ordinary, we found the fresh ones to be better than we expected.

Freshen up commercial pesto with some grated parmesan and a handful of toasted pinenuts if you have the time.

1. Bring about 5cm salted water to the boil in a medium saucepan.

2. Put chicken between two pieces kitchen paper or clingfilm and bash with the base of a saucepan until it is about 5mm thick.

3. Mix chilli with 1 tablespoon olive oil and coat the chicken. Season.

4. Simmer beans for 4 minutes or until no longer crunchy. Drain.

5. Meanwhile, heat a large frying pan or skillet. Cook chicken on a high heat for approximately 1½ minutes each side.

6. Divide chicken between plates and top with beans and pesto. Serve with lemon.

## variations:

**Vegan:** replace the chicken with slices of grilled aubergine, and use basil oil instead of the pesto.

**Vegetarian:** use tofu instead of the chicken, or finely slice halloumi and pan-fry in a little oil until golden on both sides, around 3–4 minutes.

**Short on time?** Replace the beans with mange tout and skip the cooking step.

**Dairy-free:** use basil oil or mayo instead of the pesto.

10-minute trick:

Use boiled water from the kettle to speed up the bean cooking. And make sure you bash the chicken out well so it is tender and cooks quickly.

# summer chicken stir-fry

- 400g minced chicken
- 2 medium courgettes, sliced into rounds
- 2–3 tablespoons soy sauce
- large handful basil leaves
- handful whole almonds or cashews

This is a brilliant one-pot dish that I love to serve on its own. Feel free to serve with the usual stir-fry accompaniment of steamed rice if you need something more substantial.

We're using minced chicken because it saves the chopping step and cooks much faster than larger slices of chicken. But feel free to use breasts or thighs if you prefer.

1. Heat a wok on a fierce heat.

2. Add a little oil and stir-fry the chicken until no longer pink. Remove to a clean bowl.

3. Add a little more oil and stir-fry the courgettes for a few minutes or until just starting to soften.

4. Return the chicken to the pan and season with soy. Stir-fry until chicken is cooked through.

5. Remove from heat and sprinkle over basil and nuts.

variations:

**Beef:** simply replace the chicken with minced beef.

**Vegan/vegetarian:** replace the chicken with crumbled tofu or seitan.

**Different herbs:** replace the basil with mint or coriander.

**Different veg:** replace the courgettes with any veg that will cook in a short time. Asian greens like bok choy are great, or try carrots, mange tout or sugar snap peas.

**Soy-free:** replace the soy sauce with fish sauce or oyster sauce.

# spanish chicken
## with chickpeas

serves 2

- 2 large chicken thigh fillets
- 2 teaspoons smoked paprika
- 400g can chickpeas, drained
- 250g cherry tomatoes
- small handful almonds

I have a bit of a thing for 'bashing' my meat. Not only does it make it thinner so it will cook much more quickly, it also tenderises the meat. And it's a brilliant opportunity to work out any tension from the day. Who needs boxercise?

Chicken thighs tend to be cheaper and more flavoursome than chicken breast. They're my first choice when I'm looking for boneless chicken. Feel free to substitute chicken breasts if you prefer.

1. Place chicken between 2 sheets kitchen paper and bash with the base of a saucepan until about 5mm thick.

2. Combine paprika with 2 tablespoons extra virgin olive oil and coat the chicken thoroughly. Season.

3. Heat a frying pan on medium-high heat.

4. Sear chicken for 3–4 minutes. Add chickpeas, tomatoes and almonds.

5. Turn the chicken and sear for another 3–4 minutes or until cooked through.

variations:

**Steaks:** replace the chicken with 2 steaks, preferably from grass-fed beef.

**Vegan/vegetarian:** replace the chicken with firm tofu or seitan. Slice into 'steaks' about 1cm thick rather than bashing out.

**Can't find smoked paprika?** It's really worth the effort to find some, but if you don't have any luck, just use regular Hungarian paprika.

**Greener:** serve with a green salad or some steamed greens or broccoli on the side.

**Nut-free:** replace the almonds with finely diced red peppers.

10-minute trick:

To minimise the chicken cooking time, make sure you bash it out into a thin piece. And don't stress if it tears a little.

**10-minute trick:**

This is all about getting the chicken cooked, so preheat your pan and cut the chicken as finely as possible.

# stir-fry of cashew nuts and chicken

**serves 2**

- 2 chicken breasts, finely sliced
- large handful cashew nuts
- 3 tablespoons oyster sauce
- 1 tablespoon fish sauce
- 3 spring onions, finely sliced

I ordered this the first ever time I went to a Thai restaurant. I can still remember how it blew me away with the tenderness of the chicken, the nutty crunch of the cashews and the exotic, pungent sauce. So it was only natural that it was one of the first Thai dishes I learned to cook.

Feel free to use a little sugar to season this. Traditionally it has quite a bit of sweetness, but I prefer it more salty.

1. Heat a few tablespoons olive or peanut oil in a large wok or frying pan over a high heat.

2. Stir-fry chicken and cashew nuts for a few minutes, or until chicken is just cooked through.

3. Quickly add the sauces and stir to heat through.

4. Taste and season with a little sugar if you like.

5. Remove from the heat and toss in spring onions.

**variations:**

**More substantial:** serve with steamed rice or cauliflower 'rice' (finely grated raw cauliflower).

**Vegan/vegetarian:** replace the chicken with diced tofu or seitan; mushrooms or broccoli are other lovely veggie alternatives. And either use a vegetarian 'oyster' sauce or replace with hoisin sauce, and use soy sauce instead of the fish.

**Herby:** lovely with fresh basil, mint or coriander.

# butter chicken curry

- 250g chicken thigh fillets
- 2 tablespoons garam masala
- 1–2 teaspoons chilli flakes
- 400g can tomatoes, chopped
- 2–3 tablespoons whipping cream

My first casual job at university was waitressing at a local Indian restaurant. It taught me two very important life lessons: first, I am hopeless when it comes to waiting tables, and second, that Indian food is delicious.

Butter chicken was my first Indian-food love, before I boarded the train to spice central and learned to appreciate the hot curries like vindaloo.

In restaurants, butter chicken can be super greasy. So it's much better to enjoy it at home where you can control the amount of cream you add. I also like having the freedom to turn up the chilli heat.

1. Chop chicken into chunks.

2. Heat a few tablespoons olive oil in a large frying pan over a medium-high heat.

3. Brown chicken for few minutes each side.

4. Add garam masala and chilli. Stir for a few seconds.

5. Add tomatoes and their juices. Simmer for about 5 minutes.

6. Stir in cream and bring back to simmer.

7. Taste and season with salt and pepper, and a little sugar if you like.

variations:

**Vegan:** replace the chicken with crumbled tofu or seitan, and use coconut milk instead of the cream.

**Vegetarian:** make butter chickpeas by replacing the chicken with a drained can of chickpeas.

**Dairy-free:** use coconut milk instead of the cream.

**Healthier:** feel free to reduce the cream and stir in a generous handful of baby spinach to lighten everything up.

**10-minute trick:**

This is all about getting the grill hot, so crank it up before you start gathering your ingredients.

# grilled pork kebabs

- 1 tablespoon ground cumin
- 1 tablespoon smoked paprika
- 2 cloves garlic, finely chopped
- 450g diced pork
- 4–6 tablespoons natural yoghurt

Kebabs are a great way to make meat go a little further. I've kept it simple here, but you can easily add vegetables such as mushrooms, red peppers or courgettes to the skewer to make things more interesting.

If you can't find smoked paprika, just use regular paprika.

1. Preheat an overhead grill on the highest heat. Place 4 wooden skewers in water to soak.

2. Combine cumin, paprika, most of the garlic and 3 tablespoons olive oil in a bowl. Toss in the pork to coat each piece. Thread pork onto skewers.

3. Cook pork under the grill for about 3 minutes each side, or until cooked to your liking.

4. While the pork is cooking, mix yoghurt with remaining garlic and season well.

5. Serve skewers with sauce on the side.

variations:

**Different meat:** equally good with chicken breast or good-quality steak.

**Vegan/vegetarian:** replace the pork with tofu or seitan, and use a vegan mayonnaise or hummus instead of the yoghurt.

**Dairy-free:** try vegan mayonnaise or hummus instead of the yoghurt.

# pork sausage
## with ratatouille

**serves 2**

- 2–3 Italian-style pork sausages
- 125g cherry tomatoes
- 3 grilled red peppers, sliced into ribbons
- 4 slices grilled aubergine
- small bunch flat-leaf parsley, leaves picked

This might seem like cheating, using grilled red peppers and aubergines from a jar, but there's no way you could have ratatouille cooked in anything less than half an hour if making it from scratch, and I was pleasantly surprised at the quality of the jar versions.

1. Heat 2 tablespoons olive oil in a large frying pan.

2. Remove sausage skins and crumble the meat into the pan. Cook for a few minutes, stirring, until the sausage starts to brown.

3. Add tomatoes, peppers and aubergine. Cook for 5 minutes or until the tomatoes are starting to wrinkle and the sausage is cooked.

4. Remove from the heat. Toss in parsley. Taste and season.

## variations:

**Vegetarian:** skip the sausages and serve with some cheese crumbled over at the end. A salty feta or creamy goat's cheese would be my first choices.

**Vegan:** replace the sausages with crumbled tofu or seitan.

**Leafy:** toss in a generous handful of mixed salad leaves or baby spinach for a lighter, healthier ratatouille.

**More substantial:** toss in some cooked pasta or canned beans, or serve with a good rustic sourdough and lashings of butter.

10-minute trick:
Get the sausages cooking before preparing the other ingredients.

10-minute trick:

Get the chorizo on to cook before
you do anything else.

# chorizo with chickpeas and tomato

- 2 chorizos (approx. 200g), sliced into coins
- 400g can chickpeas, drained
- 2 tablespoons smoked paprika, optional
- 250g cherry tomatoes, halved
- small bunch flat-leaf parsley, chopped

I hate to make sweeping generalisations, but I'm yet to meet a pork-eating bloke who doesn't get excited about chorizo. Ladies (and gentlemen for that matter), if you're ever looking to get a guy excited about your cooking, this is the dish to do it.

If you had more time, you could substitute some boiled new or salad potatoes for the chickpeas.

1. Heat 2 tablespoons olive oil in a frying pan on high.

2. Stir-fry chorizo until nicely brown on both sides.

3. Stir through chickpeas and paprika, if using. Cook for another minute or two.

4. Taste, season, and stir through tomatoes and parsley.

## variations:

No chorizo? Any other spicy sausage or salami will work. Streaky bacon combined with a little chilli would also be acceptable.

Vegan/vegetarian: replace the chorizo with a chopped red pepper.

Different herbs: mint, coriander and basil are also good here.

Hot! Use a hot chorizo or add a little extra dried chilli powder.

Can't find smoked paprika? Use regular paprika instead.

# lamb fillet with mint and hummus

- 2 teaspoons ground cumin
- 4 lamb fillets, finely sliced
- lemon juice
- 6–8 tablespoons hummus (see introduction)
- small bunch mint, leaves picked

I absolutely love hummus. It's one of the most useful things. It makes a wonderful dip with some pita bread, it's also lovely on sandwiches as a healthier option to butter or mayonnaise, but I think my favourite way to eat it is like this, with tender meaty lamb fillet and some fresh mint.

You can get pretty good hummus from the supermarket, but if you feel like making your own, whizz together a can of chickpeas with a clove of garlic and 3 tablespoons each of lemon juice, tahini and liquid from the chickpea can. Too easy.

1. Mix cumin with 2 tablespoons olive oil and season. Coat lamb with the oil.

2. Place a large frying pan on a medium-high heat and cook lamb for about 2 minutes, stirring every 30 seconds or so.

3. When the lamb is cooked, remove from the pan and sprinkle with a squeeze of lemon juice.

4. Divide hummus between 2 plates. Top with lamb and scatter over mint leaves.

## variations:

**Other meat:** replace the lamb with beef fillet, good-quality steak, or chicken breast or thighs.

**Vegan/vegetarian:** replace the lamb with mushrooms or aubergine, sliced and pan-fried until tender – or use grilled aubergine from the deli or a jar.

**Different herbs:** replace the mint with parsley or coriander.

**More substantial:** serve with pita bread and a green salad or tabbouleh.

10-minute trick:
Slice the lamb finely for maximum tenderness and speedy cooking.

# lamb cutlets with white-bean mash and seared tomato

serves 2

- 6–8 lamb cutlets, French trimmed
- 250g cherry tomatoes
- 2 sprigs rosemary, leaves picked
- 400g can cannellini or butter beans, drained
- 2 handfuls grated parmesan

I grew up on a sheep farm. To say we ate a lot of lamb is a massive understatement. During university I went through an anti-lamb phase, but I soon got over that when the mother of my boyfriend at the time cooked me little lamb cutlets.

Feel free to use another type of lamb chop if you are cooking on a budget, as cutlets do tend to be expensive. Lamb fillets are a great option for those who aren't into chewing on bones.

I've given the instructions for cooking in the kitchen, but feel free to barbecue or use a griddle pan if you have one.

1. Heat a few tablespoons olive oil in a medium frying pan over a high heat.

2. Season lamb and add to the pan with tomatoes and rosemary.

3. Sear for 2–3 minutes each side or until lamb is cooked to your liking.

4. Meanwhile, mash beans, parmesan and 1 tablespoon extra virgin olive oil together with a fork until you have a chunky paste. Taste and season.

5. Serve cutlets on a bed of white-bean mash with rosemary and tomatoes.

## variations:

**Budget:** use less expensive lamb chops; they may need cooking a little longer.

**Vegan:** replace the lamb with field or portobello mushrooms. Pan-fry until soft and well browned, about 5 minutes each side. Replace the parmesan with 2 tablespoons tahini.

**Different herbs:** rosemary is lovely with lamb, but thyme or lemon thyme also works.

**Healthier:** serve with a green salad or a big plate of greens.

**Vegetarian:** replace the lamb with sliced halloumi.

# quick sausage cassoulet

- 3–4 good-quality pork sausages
- 400g can tomatoes
- 400g can white beans, drained
- 1 tablespoon lemon juice
- handful baby spinach leaves

Cassoulet is a wonderful southern French peasant dish of beans and sausage, and sometimes duck and pork. A traditional cassoulet takes days to make, with the soaking and cooking of the beans and the *confit-ing* of the duck.

This super-simple version takes a tiny fraction of the time yet delivers a wonderfully satisfying meal. Just make sure you use the best quality pork sausages you can get your hands on. I've used plain pork sausages here, but something like a Toulouse sausage with a little garlic wouldn't go astray.

1. Heat a medium pan on a high heat. Add a few tablespoons olive oil.

2. Remove sausage skins and crumble the meat into chunks in the pan. Discard the skins. Fry, stirring occasionally for a few minutes, or until sausages are starting to brown on the outside.

3. Add tomatoes and bring to a simmer. Cook for another few minutes or until sausages are cooked through and the sauce is hot.

4. Add beans and bring back to a simmer. Taste. Season.

5. Toss lemon juice with 2 tablespoons extra virgin olive oil. Season and toss the spinach leaves to coat.

## variations:

**Vegetarian:** skip the sausages and serve with thin slices of brie on top. And add a few knobs of butter to the tomatoes for a little extra richness.

**Vegan:** replace the sausages with crumbled tofu or seitan.

**Different beans:** small white beans are traditional but any cooked or canned legumes will work. I love chickpeas.

**More substantial:** serve with crusty bread and butter.

# seared beef 'carpaccio' with mustard

serves 2

- 150g best-quality fillet of beef
- 2 tablespoons wholegrain mustard
- 2 tablespoons whole-egg mayonnaise
- 1 tablespoon chopped chives
- crusty bread, to serve

If you're a little nervous about serving raw beef, this slightly bastardised version of carpaccio is an excellent compromise. The beef fillet is seared on the outside and then finely sliced. The surface of the meat is the most likely source of any bugs, so by cooking the surface, you greatly reduce your risk.

1. Heat a frying pan on a very high heat.

2. Rub beef with olive oil and season. Sear beef for about 30 seconds on each side. Rest.

3. While the beef is resting, combine mustard and mayonnaise and season.

4. Slice the beef as finely as possible and layer over a serving platter.

5. Drizzle over dressing and scatter with chives. Serve with the bread.

variations:

Gluten-free: serve with a big green salad instead of the bread.

Egg-free: try hummus instead of the mustardy mayo or use vegan mayo.

Leafy: serve with a green salad.

# ginger beef stir-fry

- 300g steak, trimmed and finely sliced
- 2–3 tablespoons ginger, chopped into matchsticks
- 4–5 spring onions, sliced
- 1 bunch bok choy, sliced
- sesame oil, to serve

The older I get the more I find myself loving ginger in both sweet and savoury dishes. Many stir-fry recipes start off with the 'holy trinity' of ginger, garlic and chilli. I prefer to focus on one element at a time, but feel free to use all three seasonings if you like.

1. Heat a wok on a fierce heat.

2. Add a little oil and stir-fry the beef and ginger until the beef is no longer pink. Remove from the heat and place in a clean bowl.

3. Add the spring onion and bok choy and stir-fry until the bok choy is starting to wilt – a few minutes.

4. Return the ginger and beef to the pan. Stir-fry for another few seconds or until the beef is hot.

5. Remove from the heat. Season with salt and pepper and drizzle with sesame oil.

## variations:

**Vegan/vegetarian:** replace the beef with sliced tofu or seitan.

**Herby:** serve sprinkled with flat-leaf parsley or mint leaves.

**Hot!** Add a few finely sliced red chillies with the ginger.

**Different veg:** brussels sprouts are lovely cooked like this; also consider broccoli, cauliflower, mange tout, beans, courgettes, red peppers or even baby spinach.

**Sesame-free:** season with soy sauce instead of the salt and sesame oil.

**More substantial:** increase the amount of beef or serve with rice or noodles.

10-minute trick:

The finer you slice your courgettes the quicker they will cook.

# beef *with* buttery courgettes

- 450g minced beef
- 4 medium courgettes, sliced into thin rounds
- 1–2 teaspoons dried chilli, optional
- lemon juice, to serve

For simple week-night dinners, one-pot meals like this can be a life saver. I used to think dinner needed to have lots of different elements to be satisfying, but these days I'm just as happy with a simple, modern meat and veg combo like this.

I love the texture of minced beef when it's well cooked and crispy on the edges. The melting, buttery courgettes make a wonderful contrast. Pork, lamb or chicken mince would be equally lovely.

1. Heat a few tablespoons olive oil in a large frying pan.

2. Cook beef over medium-high heat, stirring for a minute or so.

3. Add courgettes and chilli. Continue to cook, stirring every now and then.

4. When the meat is well browned and the courgettes are soft and buttery, remove from the heat.

5. Squeeze over 2–3 tablespoons lemon juice. Taste and season generously with salt and pepper.

variations:

**Different meat:** any minced meat is good here. Try chicken, pork, turkey, buffalo or even kangaroo!

**Vegan/vegetarian:** replace the beef with crumbled tofu or seitan, and add a little ground cumin or coriander for extra flavour.

**Herby:** add a little freshness with a handful of basil, mint or parsley.

**More substantial:** toss in a drained can of legumes or some cooked pasta, or serve on a bed of either mashed potato or cauliflower purée.

# salt-crusted burger

- 250g minced beef
- 1 tablespoon tomato ketchup
- 4 tablespoons mayonnaise
- 2 English muffins, halved
- lettuce

This is a great method for cooking burgers when you don't have access to a barbecue. The thin layer of salt helps form a lovely crust on the burger and stops juices being lost. It can be quite salty though, so be sparing with the amount of salt you use.

Feel free to use whichever condiments you prefer. This mayo and ketchup mixture may look a little too pink, but it tastes delicious.

1. Preheat a frying pan on a very high heat.

2. Form beef into two burger patties.

3. Scatter the surface of the pan with 1 scant teaspoon of fine sea salt.

4. Sear burgers for 3–4 minutes on each side or until cooked to your liking.

5. Mix ketchup with the mayonnaise and spread on the insides of both muffins.

6. Place a burger on each muffin and top with the lettuce and remaining muffin halves.

## variations:

**Different meats:** replace the beef with minced chicken.

**Vegan/vegetarian:** see the minimalist lentil burger on page 164.

**Short on time?** Form the meat into 4 thin burger patties so they cook faster and then serve 2 patties per person.

**Budget:** replace up to a quarter of the beef with fresh breadcrumbs.

**Egg-free:** skip the mayo and serve with ketchup or barbecue sauce.

**10-minute trick:**

It's important to get the pan as hot as possible so that your burger cooks quickly and forms a nice crust. Lower temperatures may result in your burger sticking.

# lebanese beef *and* hummus *with* cucumber salad

serves 2–3

- 450g minced beef
- 3–4 teaspoons baharat or ground cumin
- 2 cucumbers
- ½ a lemon
- 6–8 tablespoons hummus

I just love the combination of well-browned spiced beef on a bed of smooth, smooth hummus. Add a cooling cucumber salad and you've got a meal in minutes!

Feel free to use good-quality store-bought hummus, or make your own: my favourite recipe is to drain a can of chickpeas, reserving 3 tablespoons of the liquid, whizz both with a clove of garlic or two and 3 tablespoons each of lemon juice and tahini. Too easy.

1. Heat a large frying pan on a high heat. Add a few tablespoons oil and the beef. Stir-fry for a few minutes.

2. Add baharat and continue to cook beef, stirring occasionally until really well browned. Taste and season.

3. Meanwhile, shave the outside layers of the cucumber into ribbons, discarding the watery seeds in the centre. Toss ribbons in a bowl with a little salt and a squeeze of lemon.

4. To serve, smear hummus over the base of your plates. Top with hot beef and arrange salad on the side.

## variations:

**Different meat:** this is also lovely with lamb or chicken.

**Vegan/vegetarian:** replace the beef with 2 drained cans of lentils.

**Budget:** either try the vegetarian option or replace half the beef with lentils.

**Cucumber-free:** replace the cucumber with courgettes or a few generous handfuls of washed baby spinach leaves.

# beef tonnato

- 185g tuna in oil, drained
- 8 tablespoons whole-egg mayonnaise
- 6 tablespoons lemon juice + zest of 1 lemon
- 350g sliced roast beef from the deli
- 2–3 handfuls rocket leaves

This recipe was inspired by the classic Italian dish *vitello tonnato*. The tonnato refers to the tuna mayonnaise used to dress the finely sliced poached veal. In this 10-minute version, we're skipping the poaching and chilling of the veal and picking up some cold roast beef from the deli. A million times easier but just as delicious.

Even if you're not a massive tuna fan, I really encourage you to try this. It's just wonderful how the richly flavoured mayo complements the beef. Any leftovers make a super delicious sandwich filling – actually you may find yourself making extra to make sure you have some leftovers.

1. Place tuna in a bowl and mash with a fork to remove any chunks.

2. Stir in the mayo, lemon juice and zest. Taste and season.

3. Tear beef into bite-sized pieces and toss in the dressing.

4. Arrange beef on a platter or wooden chopping board and scatter rocket leaves on the side.

variations:

**Vegan/vegetarian:** replace the tuna with a small drained can of chickpeas and the beef with finely sliced field mushrooms (roast with butter or oil at 180°C for about 30 minutes until tender).

**Fish-free:** replace the tuna with a small drained can of chickpeas.

**More substantial:** serve with rustic sourdough bread.

**Egg-free:** use a vegan or 'egg-free' mayonnaise.

# super simple sang choi bau

serves 2

- 250g minced beef
- 225g can water chestnuts, drained
- 1–2 teaspoons dried chilli flakes
- 4 tablespoons oyster sauce
- 6 leaves iceberg lettuce

One of my friends is from Texas. He is convinced that sang choi bau is the perfect food because you could live on it alone, if you had to. He does have a point. The combination of richly sauced meat with crunchy water chestnuts wrapped in a crisp, refreshing lettuce-leaf parcel is hard to beat.

The recipe below yields two moderately sized servings. If you're feeding a particularly hungry carnivore, it might be a good idea to double the recipe.

1. Heat a few tablespoons olive oil in a large frying pan.

2. Cook beef and water chestnuts, stirring frequently, until the beef is well browned and cooked through.

3. Add chilli and oyster sauce and 2 tablespoons water. Cook until everything is hot.

4. Taste and season.

5. Serve hot beef in a bowl with lettuce leaves for wrapping on the side.

## variations:

**Different meat:** pork is commonly used but you could also make your sang choi bau from minced chicken or turkey.

**Vegan/vegetarian:** replace the beef with a drained can of lentils and use a vegetarian 'oyster' sauce or hoisin sauce.

**Fish-free:** use a vegetarian 'oyster' sauce, hoisin sauce or sweet soy sauce.

**Budget:** replace some or all of the meat with canned lentils.

# minute steak *with* chilli oil *and* broccolini

- 1 bunch broccolini
- 2 tablespoons lemon juice
- 2 steaks about 1cm thick
- 1 teaspoon chilli flakes

Flavoured oils aren't something that I use very often. But they do make a wonderful instant sauce when served on top of something hot, like here, on freshly cooked meat and greens.

If chilli isn't your thing you could try some horseradish oil or mix finely chopped anchovies into the oil. For some reason the anchovies make the meat taste meatier, rather than fishy. Be brave and try it some time.

1. Bring a medium saucepan of salted water to the boil. Cook broccolini for 5 minutes or until tender. Drain and toss with lemon juice.

2. Meanwhile, using the base of a saucepan, bash steaks out until they are half the thickness. Rub with olive oil and season.

3. Preheat a frying pan on a high heat. Sear steaks for a minute on each side, or until cooked to your liking. Rest on 2 warm dinner plates.

4. Combine chilli with 2 tablespoons extra virgin olive oil.

5. Serve steaks topped with broccolini and chilli oil.

variations:

**Vegan:** replace the steaks with sliced tofu or seitan.

**Vegetarian:** use sliced halloumi cheese instead of the steaks.

**Different veg:** try regular broccoli, purple-sprouting broccoli or asparagus.

**Fresh chilli:** replace the chilli flakes with 1–3 finely chopped fresh red chillies.

*10-minute trick:*

Both the broccolini and the steak are going to take some time, so focus on these and leave the chilli oil until last.

**10-minute trick:**

It's important to get the pan as hot as possible so that your burger cooks quickly and forms a nice crust. Lower temperatures may result in your burger sticking.

# 'european' beef burgers
## with red wine sauce

- 400g minced beef
- small glass red wine
- 2–3 tablespoons tomato paste
- 2 generous tablespoons butter
- mixed salad leaves, to serve

Everyone loves a burger – there are few more economical and reliably tender cuts of meat. But sometimes you need something a bit less snacky for dinner. These burgers were inspired by a meal I had in the beautiful city of Barcelona, where they served a burger patty with salad and a fancy sauce. So I've called these burgers 'European' to capture that feeling.

1. Preheat a large frying pan on very high heat.

2. Form beef into 2 patties.

3. Sprinkle a scant teaspoon salt on the hot pan and place burgers on top.

4. Sear burgers for about 4 minutes on each side. Remove meat and rest on 2 warm dinner plates.

5. Add wine and tomato paste to the pan. Simmer for a minute or so, stirring to scrape up any burger bits into the sauce.

6. Stir in butter until melted. Taste and season sauce.

7. Serve burgers with sauce poured over and green salad on the side.

## variations:

**Different meat:** also good with chicken.

**Vegan/vegetarian:** use the lentil burger recipe on page 164 and see below for a butter alternative.

**Budget:** replace up to a quarter of the beef with soft breadcrumbs or cooked lentils.

**Alcohol-free:** replace the wine with 1 tablespoon wine vinegar.

**Dairy-free:** skip the butter and use 6 tablespoons of tomato passata or a commercial tomato pasta sauce instead of the more intense tomato paste.

# mexican beef *and* refried beans

serves 2–3

- 450g minced beef
- 1–2 teaspoons chilli powder
- 375g jar salsa
- ½ an iceberg lettuce
- 400g can refried beans

I keep forgetting about refried beans but when I remember, I just love them! Great flavour and creamy texture to contrast with crispy iceberg lettuce.

Using salsa as a sauce for ground beef was a new one for me. I really loved the results: fresh and very different from the Italian flavour-profile of good old spag bol without taking much time.

1. Heat a large frying pan on a high heat. Add a few tablespoons oil and the beef. Stir-fry for a few minutes.

2. Add chilli and continue to cook, stirring occasionally, until really well browned.

3. Add salsa and reduce heat to a simmer. Cook, stirring occasionally, for about 5 minutes or until the sauce is hot and reduced slightly. Taste and season.

4. Meanwhile, rinse, dry and finely shred the lettuce.

5. To serve, smear a layer of beans over the base of your plates. Top with hot beef and serve with lettuce on the side.

variations:

**Vegan/vegetarian:** replace the beef with crumbled tofu or seitan.

**Different lettuce:** if iceberg isn't your thing, serve with baby spinach or other washed salad leaves. Fresh coriander leaves are also great.

**Can't find refried beans?** Just replace with a drained can of white beans or red kidney beans puréed with a few tablespoons extra virgin olive oil.

**No salsa?** Use a commercial tomato pasta sauce instead.

# steak with ricotta and red peppers

- 2 steaks, about 1cm thick
- 4 roasted red peppers, cut into ribbons
- 200g ricotta
- 1 tablespoon lemon juice
- 2 large handfuls mixed salad leaves

The best trick for cooking steaks in a hurry is to flatten them with the base of a saucepan until they are about 5mm thick. This not only allows them to cook in a minute on each side, it also tenderises the steak, so the cheaper, more flavoursome cuts like rump are ideal. I love this with sirloin steaks as well, but my favourite would have to be rib-eye off the bone.

I've written the instructions below for cooking in a pan, but feel free to use your barbecue or a griddle pan.

1. Using the base of a saucepan, bash steaks out until they are half the thickness. Rub with olive oil. Season.

2. Preheat a frying pan on very high heat.

3. Sear steaks for a minute on each side, or until cooked to your liking. Remove from the pan and rest on warm dinner plates.

4. Cook peppers for a minute or until heated through.

5. Place a dollop of ricotta on each steak and top with warm peppers.

6. Mix lemon juice with 2 tablespoons extra virgin olive oil and dress leaves.

## variations:

**Vegetarian:** replace the steaks with large field mushrooms. They'll need about 5 minutes on each side.

**Vegan:** use mushrooms instead of the steaks and hummus instead of the ricotta.

**Hot!** Serve with a drizzle of chilli oil or add 1–2 finely chopped red chillies to cook with the peppers.

**Budget:** use smaller steaks or try beef sausages instead.

# sweet treats

# chocolate 'ice magic'

- 50g best-quality dark chocolate
- 2 tablespoons boiling water
- 2 generous scoops vanilla ice cream

When I was little, there was this chocolate sauce called Ice Magic which you poured over ice cream and left to set to give a crunchy chocolate topping. The chocolate flavour was always a bit fake, but we were prepared to overlook that on account of the crunch.

But now I've found a solution. A simple chocolate sauce that is 100% chocolatey goodness without any crazy additives. Just the thing for when you feel like an unexpected sweet treat and only have chocolate and ice cream in the house. This is also great served with cakes or puddings.

1. Break chocolate into small pieces in a heatproof bowl.

2. Pour over boiling water and allow to stand for a few minutes.

3. Stir until chocolate is melted and you have a smooth sauce.

4. Drizzle sauce over ice cream.

## variations:

**Dairy-free/vegan:** either use a dairy-free ice cream or try a coconut sorbet.

**Milk chocolate:** feel free to use your favourite milk chocolate if you prefer.

**Double choc:** replace the vanilla ice cream with a chocolate ice cream.

**Honeycomb:** use a honeycomb ice cream or smash your favourite honeycomb chocolate bar and stir into the vanilla ice cream before topping with the melted chocolate.

# (almost) instant apple crumble

serves 4

- 4 tablespoons butter
- 770g can sliced apples
- 8 digestive biscuits or oatmeal cookies, finely chopped
- 80g whole almonds, roughly chopped
- vanilla ice cream, to serve

This is one of those recipes that your guests probably won't believe you whipped up in 10 minutes. So probably best to just keep that between you and me.

It's pretty amazing what you can do with a can of sliced apples, a packet of biscuits and some almonds.

1. Melt half the butter in a large frying pan over a high heat.

2. Add drained apple. Stir-fry until apple is warm and a little browned at the edges, approximately 4 minutes.

3. Divide apple between 4 ramekins or other plain serving bowls. Keep warm.

4. Melt remaining butter over a high heat. Stir-fry biscuits and almonds until golden.

5. Sprinkle mixture over the apple and serve immediately with ice cream.

variations:

**Dairy-free/vegan:** either use a dairy-free ice cream or try a coconut sorbet to serve, and use a neutral flavoured oil instead of the butter.

**Gluten-free:** use gluten-free biscuits.

**Nut-free:** skip the nuts and increase the biscuits slightly.

**Different fruit:** lovely with canned pears or peaches.

# vanilla poached apricots with ice cream

- 1 tablespoon sugar
- ½ a vanilla pod, seeds scraped out
- 200g dried apricots
- vanilla ice cream, to serve

I love apricots, but even when they are in season it can be difficult to find one perfectly ripe and full of flavour. So I tend to avoid the risk of a dud fresh apricot and use dried.

This dessert is super simple, but there's something beautiful about the way the ice cream melts into the sweet vanilla sauce.

1. Bring sugar, 125ml water, vanilla pod and seeds to the boil in a medium saucepan.

2. Stir until sugar is dissolved, then add the apricots.

3. Simmer for about 5 minutes or until apricots are lovely and plump.

4. Serve warm or cold with a generous scoop of vanilla ice cream.

variations:

**Vegan:** use whipped coconut cream or coconut sorbet instead of the ice cream.

**Different fruit:** lovely with dates or prunes instead.

**Breakfast:** serve the apricots with yoghurt and muesli.

**Budget:** skip the vanilla bean and use ½ teaspoon of vanilla extract.

**Healthier:** replace the ice cream with a good-quality natural yoghurt.

# speedy summer puddings

serves 2

- 100g berries + extra to serve
- 2 tablespoons caster sugar
- 2 slices white bread
- vanilla ice cream, to serve

Such a brilliantly named dessert and such a refreshing one as well. Traditionally, summer pudding is bread and berries, left overnight for the bread to soak up all the juices. The texture of this 10-minute version is less bready and more berry, which I actually like a bit better.

Use the sugar quantity in the recipe as a guide. If you think it needs more sweetness, by all means adjust.

Vanilla ice cream is my go-to dessert accompaniment. But feel free to mix it up with clotted cream, mascarpone or even some good old softly whipped cream.

1. Mash berries together with sugar until dissolved.

2. Cut 2 circles from each slice of bread by pushing a cookie cutter or small wine glass down on the bread.

3. Squish bread into the berry mixture until each circle is lovely and pink. Place bread into 2 small glasses, tea cups or ramekins, using two circles for each pudding.

4. Scatter over extra berries and drizzle over any remaining berry–sugar mixture.

variations:

Dairy-free/vegan: serve with whipped coconut cream: chill a can of coconut milk then spoon off the solid 'cream' from the top and whip as you would regular cream.

Gluten-free: crumble some sweet gluten-free cookies into the glasses and top with the berries. Frozen berries are excellent here – just defrost before using.

Different berries: I've used raspberries but feel free to use a mixture of different berries.

# crunchy bread puddings

serves 2

- 60g caster sugar
- 125ml whipping cream
- 1 egg
- 2 thick slices bread, cut into cubes
- cream or ice cream, to serve

Bread and butter pudding is one of my all-time favourite winter desserts. So I challenged myself to come up with a 10-minute version for the book. I really surprised myself with these little beauties – they tick all the boxes.

I've served them with cream here, but they would be even better with melting vanilla ice cream.

I love that this recipe only makes two servings. No need to worry about evil, tempting left-over dessert in the morning. Yay.

Having said that, it should be fine to double the recipe if needed, but any more than that and you'll probably struggle to fit everything under the grill.

1. Preheat your overhead grill to its hottest.

2. Combine sugar, cream and egg in a small bowl.

3. Squash bread cubes into the egg mixture to soak up as much as possible.

4. Place everything on a foil-lined tray and cook under the grill for 5 minutes.

5. Turn and cook the other side of the bread for another 3 minutes or until golden-brown.

6. Divide between two small bowls and serve with cream or ice cream.

variations:

Dairy-free/vegan: use coconut cream instead of the whipping cream and egg.

Gluten-free: choose a gluten-free bread.

Cinnamon: add a ½ teaspoon ground cinnamon to the sugar–egg mixture.

Egg-free: replace the cream, sugar and egg with a commercial egg-free custard.

# fresh pineapple
## *with* mint sugar

- ½ a ripe pineapple, chilled
- 1–2 tablespoons sugar
- 3 sprigs mint, leaves picked and chopped

There are few better ways to end a long, lazy summer lunch than with a platter of fresh pineapple straight from the fridge. Sprinkled with a little mint and sugar, it's one of those desserts that feels like you've gone to a bit of effort when really you haven't.

I love the fresh clean flavours – just the thing to satisfy any cravings for something sweet without being too filling.

1. Cut the pineapple in half lengthwise, then cut off the skin and any sharp bits. Be ruthless.

2. Slice into half moons about 5mm thick and lay on a serving platter.

3. Mash sugar and mint together in a small bowl or mortar and pestle.

4. Sprinkle over the pineapple and serve immediately or chill until needed.

## variations:

**Healthier:** skip the sugar and serve with a squeeze of lime instead.

**Melon:** replace the pineapple with super-ripe melon such as canteloupe.

**Simple:** don't worry about the mint.

**Richer:** serve with a big scoop of vanilla ice cream or coconut sorbet.

# french toast with raspberry sauce

- 1 egg
- 5 tablespoons sugar
- 2 slices rustic bread
- 150g raspberries
- vanilla ice cream, to serve

While french toast makes a fabulous breakfast, it can also moonlight effectively as a dessert creature. Just dress it up with a little raspberry sauce and ice cream.

I like to use rustic sourdough for my toast, but brioche would make a lovely, more decadent alternative.

1. Preheat an overhead grill.

2. Mix egg with 2 tablespoons sugar and push the bread into the mixture to soak up as much as possible.

3. Cook bread under the grill for about 8 minutes, turning every few minutes until the toast is golden-brown and puffy.

4. Meanwhile, make the sauce. Mash berries together with the other 3 tablespoons of sugar.

5. Serve toast warm with sauce drizzled over and topped with a generous scoop of ice cream.

variations:

**Gluten-free:** use gluten-free bread.

**Egg-free:** replace egg with 4 tablespoons cream.

**Dairy-free:** serve with whipped coconut cream.

**Different berries:** don't feel limited to raspberries – blackberries, blueberries or even a mixture of berries would be wonderful.

10-minute trick:

Soften the biscuits in the microwave for about 20 seconds instead of preheating your oven.

# little ricotta tartlets with fig and honey

## serves 2

- 250g ricotta
- 2 tablespoons sugar
- 8 digestive biscuits
- 2 large ripe figs, quartered lengthwise
- honey

Make sure you get your ricotta from a good deli and don't use the watery ricotta they sell in tubs in the supermarket.

You could use any fruit you like. If figs aren't in season try fresh berries or finely sliced ripe pears, or you could even go tropical with sliced mango and passionfruit. And it's not limited to fruit toppings – try praline, chopped nuts, even shaved chocolate. I need to make these tarts again soon.

1. Preheat oven to 200°C.

2. Meanwhile, combine ricotta and sugar in a small bowl.

3. Place 4 biscuits in the oven for 2 minutes.

4. Remove from the oven. Using a soup spoon and a tea towel, carefully shape the biscuits into little tartlet shells.

5. Repeat with remaining biscuits.

6. Divide ricotta mixture between tartlet shells.

7. Top each with a fig quarter and drizzle with honey.

## variations:

**Gluten-free:** use gluten-free biscuits, and skip the warming and shaping step as they'll be more likely to break.

**Dairy-free/vegan:** use whipped coconut cream in place of the ricotta. Vegans who don't eat honey can use maple syrup instead.

**Short on time?** Don't worry about warming and shaping the biscuits – just serve them flat with ricotta and figs on top.

# mixed berry sorbet

- 150g frozen mixed berries
- 3 tablespoons caster sugar

I tend to keep a packet of frozen berries in the freezer for when I need a quick dessert. This berry sorbet is wonderfully simple – just whizz the berries with a little sugar in the food processor and there you have it, instant sorbet.

1. Place berries and sugar in a food processor with 1 tablespoon water.

2. Whizz until the sugar is dissolved and you have a nice shiny sorbet. It might take a little while for the berries to defrost enough to liquefy.

3. Serve immediately or keep in the freezer until you're ready – but no more than a few hours or it will start to go icy.

variations:

**Healthier:** skip the sugar.

**Ice creamy:** replace water with a few tablespoons of double cream.

**Different fruit:** frozen mango and banana both work well. Just peel and chop the fruit before freezing.

# 'caramelised' pears *with* vanilla ice cream

serves 2

- 4 halves tinned pears
- small knob butter
- 2 generous scoops vanilla ice cream
- 2–3 tablespoons brown sugar

When I was little we had dessert almost every night. It usually involved ice cream; sometimes we'd also have some tinned fruit. This recipe steps that combination up a notch by warming the fruit under the grill and giving it a bit of instant caramelisation with a touch of brown sugar. Yum.

1. Preheat an overhead grill on its highest setting.

2. Place pears, flat side up, on a baking tray and divide butter between them.

3. Grill the pears for about 5 minutes or until starting to brown on the surface.

4. Divide ice cream between two small bowls. Top with pears and sprinkle with brown sugar.

## variations:

**Dairy-free/vegan:** serve with whipped coconut cream or coconut sorbet instead of the ice cream. And replace the butter with a neutral flavoured oil.

**Short on time?** Skip the grilling and the butter and serve at room temperature with the ice cream and brown sugar.

**Different fruit:** lovely with canned peaches.

**Extra crunch:** sprinkle over some roast chopped nuts.

# little ricotta *and* milk chocolate puddings

- 60g best-quality milk chocolate, chopped
- 150g full fat ricotta

This dessert is almost too simple to write a recipe for. But don't let that sway you from trying it. I love how the ricotta and chocolate mix as you eat, so every mouthful is different, some cheesy and a little bit salty, others pure, chocolatey indulgence.

If you're a chocolate purist and can't handle the thought of using anything but 70% cocoa chocolate, please go ahead. You'll need to sweeten the ricotta with a little icing sugar first.

1. In a medium saucepan, bring 2cm water to the boil .

2. Place chocolate chunks in a bowl large enough to fit over the saucepan without the bottom of the bowl touching the water.

3. Remove saucepan from the heat and place bowl over the top. Stand for 5 minutes.

4. Meanwhile, divide ricotta between two little cups or glasses.

5. Stir chocolate, which should be melted and smooth, and spoon over the ricotta.

variations:

**Dairy-free/vegan:** use dark chocolate, and either use a dairy-free ice cream or try a coconut sorbet instead of the ricotta.

**Double choc:** replace the ricotta with chocolate ice cream.

**Honeycomb:** smash your favourite honeycomb chocolate bar and stir into the ricotta before topping with the melted chocolate.

# strawberries with balsamic and mascarpone

serves 2–4

- 2 tablespoons white sugar
- 2 tablespoons aged balsamic vinegar
- 250g strawberries
- mascarpone or thick cream, to serve

Strawberries picked fresh from the garden are a thing of beauty. Unfortunately, I find that commercially grown strawberries hardly ever come close. This is where a little sugar and balsamic vinegar can make all the difference. It may sound a little weird, but it's amazing how the balsamic intensifies the flavour of less-than-perfect strawbs.

1. Combine sugar and vinegar in a small bowl. Don't stress if the sugar doesn't dissolve, it will once it mixes with the strawberry juices.

2. Remove the tops from the strawberries and slice lengthwise.

3. Toss with the vinegar mixture. Serve with mascarpone or cream.

variations:

**Dairy-free/vegan:** serve with whipped coconut cream instead of the mascarpone.

**Different berries:** strawberries are best; raspberries would be my second choice.

**No aged balsamic?** If you only have access to inexpensive supermarket balsamic, halve the amount and replace with extra sugar.

# fresh dates *with* blue cheese

- 4–6 fresh dates
- 4–6 tablespoons creamy blue cheese

So simple, it hardly needs a recipe. But don't fall into the trap of thinking that simple means they're not special. Every time I serve these little sweet and salty treats they get rave reviews.

Feel free to explore other cheeses. Pretty much any creamy cheese will work here: mascarpone, goat's cheese, ricotta are all good.

Another even easier option is to serve the dates and cheese in the middle of the table and let everyone stuff their own.

1. Cut dates down one side and remove stone.

2. Smash a little blue cheese in to fill the hole.

3. Refrigerate until you're ready to serve.

variations:

**Vegan/dairy-free:** stuff the dates with whole pecans or almonds, or use a good crunchy peanut, almond or cashew nut butter instead of the cheese.

# little lemon cheesecakes

serves 2

- 2 shortbread or other plain sweet biscuits
- 125g mascarpone
- 4 tablespoons lemon curd

As much as I'm a die-hard baked cheesecake fan, sometimes I like to whip up something much quicker.

If you can't find mascarpone, use regular cream cheese, but you might need to get out the food processor to make sure it combines smoothly with the lemon curd.

1. Place shortbread in a plastic bag and bash with a rolling pin or something heavy until they are coarsely crumbled.

2. Divide between two small tea cups or pretty glasses.

3. Combine mascarpone and lemon curd in a bowl. Taste, and add a little more lemon curd if it needs more kick – or add a little more mascarpone if you'd like it to be creamier.

4. Divide lemon cream between the tea cups and refrigerate until you're ready to eat.

## variations:

**Vegan/dairy-free:** use whipped coconut cream instead of the mascarpone, or replace it entirely with extra lemon curd. They'll be quite intense so you may want to serve with some coconut sorbet.

**Different flavours:** use passionfruit or lime curd instead of the lemon.

**Gluten-free:** replace the biscuits with 4 tablespoons of ground almonds or pecans.

**Budget:** try regular cream cheese instead of the mascarpone.

# index

# a big thank you

To my mum, for teaching me just how important good food is in life. And more importantly that good food need not be complicated or time-consuming. I miss you. So wish you were around to see this book.

To my dashing fiancé, my Irishman, GB. Every day I am thankful for your love, friendship, laughter, inspiration, support and good tunes. There's never a dull moment with you. I'm super excited about our plans for the future and am looking forward to growing old together at our table.

To my family: Dad, Dom, Batgirl, Sas, Craig, Jack, Maddie, Bridgette, Naomi, Joel and Jemima. Thanks for all the support, love and laughter and for being crazy in a good way. I wouldn't have it any other way. Love you!

To my mates for all your support, encouragement and friendship. Especially Melissa Kingham, Jo Till, Laura Clarke, Adrian Cruttenden, Malin Larson, Rob Benz, Heidi Swain, Kate Breen, Cait Ryan, Jac Hayden, Amanda Ledger, Rhys Connery, Agnes Chan, Geoff Dowell, Robyn and Hugh Murray, Lorena Di Carlo, Trudy Lynch, Will and Caroline Jardine, Margot Andersen, Keir Semmens, Paula Smith, Anthony Mitchell, Roenna McKay, Colette de Bruyn, Toby Stephens, Penney Everitt, Paula Kennedy and Kathi Smith.

To the lovely Lindsey Evans for finding me out on the internet and seeing the potential. And to James Blackman, Emma Brown and the rest of the Penguin team for doing what you guys do best. To my agents, Danielle Svetcov and Caspian Dennis, for making the business side of things completely effortless.

To whomever invented the internet. If it wasn't for you, this book wouldn't exist and I wouldn't be making a living doing what I love most. I can't thank you enough.

Lastly, to all the readers and especially the email subscribers of my blog, www.thestone-soup.com. A huge shout of thanks for all the support, comments and questions. The thing that inspires me most is getting emails from you guys sharing how Stonesoup and my recipes have helped you become happier, healthier cooks. Thank you.